My Mom and the Frog

On the Trail of Peter Gorman

James Michael McCoy

Tater Hill Books

For Peter Gorman

And to those who knew him and traveled with him to Amazonia on jungle jaunts or through his books and stories.

For George Wada and Tom Huckabee

Without your friendship I would not have traveled to Amazonia to make a film.

For my Mom, Phyllis Marie Parker McCoy

You were always my biggest supporter.
You taught me to never give up.
You were my greatest teacher.
Love you.

Writing this book was therapy for me. I thought I had finished writing it several times, only to have the universe let me know each time that it was not complete. The years I spent working on it allowed me time to process what I had witnessed. Things are a lot different now than when I began writing this book. My Mom left us at the beginning of this year, and Peter has been gone for three years now. My friends Tom Huckabee and George Wada have also gone on to the other side. These people played a major part in the journey of creating this book. I would not have gone to Peru as a crew of one to make a documentary in the middle of Northwest Amazonia without their encouragement and support. I dedicate this book to them.

I want to thank Valerie Vande Panne for helping me edit this book. She knew Peter Gorman since his days at *High Times* magazine, and she helped me filter through a lot of information for this book. I also want to thank Sam England for designing the cover, and the maps of Peru and South America. I learned a lot about jungle medicines during the process of filming the documentary, *More Joy, Less Pain: The Life of Peter Gorman*, and there was a lot that happened during the making of the film that could not be explained in a ninety minute documentary. This book is the result of studying the giant monkey tree frog, and the use of jungle medicines in the modern world over the last ten years. The names of some individuals have been changed to protect their privacy. People are people, and if you put some of them down the way they are, they likely wouldn't be happy. Its facts are factual and the things it says happened did happen. I wrote this book for the jungle rats out there like me, and by jungle rats I mean those who seek out adventures, and are not afraid to do what's necessary to find happiness and peace.

I wrote this book with the best information that I had at the time. I interviewed a lot of people about their experiences with jungle medicines. I went directly to the source, studying the indigenous traditions in Northwest Amazonia. My work includes notes from three trips to Peru with Peter Gorman, and my experiences of making a film in the world's largest rainforest. I am grateful to include stories about my Mom's life, and how jungle medicines helped her during the last years of her life. Terence McKenna was right when he said, "Nature loves courage. You make the commitment, and nature will respond to that commitment by removing impossible obstacles. Dream the impossible dream and the world will not grind you under, it will lift you up."

I hope these stories inspire you to step out into the world to find adventure.

James Michael McCoy

Dr. Mark Plotkin wrote in *Medicine Quest: In Search of Nature's Healing Secrets:*

Twenty years ago, I stumbled across the most moving account of this ongoing tragedy that I have ever seen--and it was all because of an earache.

A common and painful ailment suffered by researchers working in the rain forest is fungal infection of the ear. The hot and wet environment of the tropics turns eardrums into petri dishes ripe for the cultivation of fungal invaders. When I began working in the Amazon in the late 1970s, I developed these infections on such a regular basis that before departing I would schedule appointments to have my ears examined at the university clinic upon my return to the States. I quickly learned that if I mentioned my occupation to the physician on duty, she or he would often tell me at great length that ethnobotany was what they really wanted to do with their careers but that they had student loans, a mortgage, a family, and so on, which was why they had been unable to pursue their dream.

I vividly remember going into the clinic with a terrible earache after an expedition to the jungles of southern Venezuela. After examining my ear, attending physician Dr. Jonathan Strongin asked if I had any idea where I might have picked up such a peculiar fungus. "Sure," I replied, "I've just returned from South America."

He asked what I had been doing south of the border, and I gave a distinctly noncommittal replay. He said,"You know, I lived with Indians in the Peruvian Amazon for several years, while I was doing my Ph.D. in anthropology, which is how I became interested in healing."

Intrigued, I made a mental note of his name, looked up his dissertation, and found one of the most poignant statements ever recorded on the inextricable interrelationship between people, plants, healing, and belief:

Since the time of their initial contact, the missionaries have openly, discouraged the shamans, viewing them as Anti-Christs. Another anthropologist reported that in the Shimaa region there was a powerful shaman who had to abandon his craft because he felt he no longer had the support of the Machiguenga people in his area. The shaman used ayahuasca to take the form of a bird to travel far and wide at a great height to discern the cause of illness. However he felt that because the missionaries had so successfully eroded the traditional faith of his people, he could no longer continue to cure. For without the faith of the population, while in the avian form he would not be able to return to his body and would crash in the forest far from his home.

Contents

Part I: The Analysis

Chapter 1
17
Chapter 2
41
Chapter 3
78
Chapter 4
103

Part II: The Teachings

Chapter 5
137
Chapter 6
160
Chapter 7
185
Chapter 8
219
Chapter 9
241

I believe in the power of books.
- Larry McMurtry

Sapo/Kambo or any jungle medicines mentioned in this book are not FDA Approved treatments for any medical conditions. This content is for educational and entertainment purposes only. It is not medical advice, and always consult with a qualified health care professional before making any decisions about your health or starting any medical treatments.

Fitzcarraldo:
To your dogs' chef! To Verdi! To Rossini! To Caruso!
Do Araujo:
To Fitzcarraldo, the conquistador of the useless!
Fitzcarraldo:
As truly as I stand here before you, someday I shall bring Grand Opera to the jungle! I will outnumber you! I will outbillion you! I am the grand spectacle in the forest! I am the inventor of rubber! Only through me will rubber become a word!

- Dialogue from the film *Fitzcarraldo*

What greatness had not floated on the ebb of that river into the mystery of the unknown earth! The dreams of men, the seed of commonwealths, the germs of empires.

Joseph Conrad
Heart of Darkness

Part I
The Analysis

1
WHO THE HELL IS PETER GORMAN?

I am simply not afraid. It's not in my dictionary of belief.
- Werner Herzog

Peter Thomas Gorman was born on February 12, 1951 in Queens, New York. He grew up in the Whitestone neighborhood of Queens. Dutch settlers named the neighborhood Whitestone, because the town was built on top of white limestone. It is the northernmost part of Queens along the East River. Peter said that when he grew up there families had three acres each, and it was mostly farmland back then. These days it's an upper class residential neighborhood. Peter was the fourth of six children in a lower middle class Irish Catholic family. He had an older brother, Michael, and four sisters Barbara, Patty, Peggy, and Regina. Peter was in and out of hospitals as a child with rheumatoid arthritis, and in those hospital beds he dreamed of going on adventures around the world. Peter's dad Thomas was a broadway actor who performed in numerous Shakespeare plays. Thomas also appeared in seven big Broadway shows, and was a joke writer for Arthur Godfrey, a popular radio, and television entertainer in the mid 1950s who was known as 'The Old Redhead.' Godfrey was famously known as the pitchman for Chesterfield cigarettes, and his slogan was, "Buy 'em by the carton". Peter smoked as many cigarettes as anyone I had ever met. He told me that he smoked two, sometimes three packs of cigarettes a day for over sixty years.

Thomas also did a lot of uncredited work in TV shows and movies, and performed as an uncredited stenographer in Sidney Lumet's *12 Angry Men* starring Henry Fonda. Peter's mom Madeline was an actress who performed on Broadway and radio, and at one time had her own Broadway show, before the demands of raising six children stopped her dreams of performing. Madeline was also a part-time lingerie model for the *New York Times*. Peter had to fend for himself at a very young age, and he was sure that his parents gave him a few bucks here and there, but it didn't happen a lot. There was never enough money to go around, so everybody had to take care of themselves. Money was tight in the Gorman house with eight people living on a working actor's salary. That's just the way it was. Peter had a paper route at eight years old, and he never stopped hustling. When Peter turned eighteen, he missed out being drafted into the Vietnam War because a guy in the military psychological unit gave him, and a dozen other longhairs death sentences on their medical reports. They told Peter that he had a brain aneurysm, and that he was going to be dead in three weeks. After receiving his death assessment, Peter ran into a few other longhairs in the parking lot who had also received death sentences. They all received four F's on their medical examinations that day. Peter believed that several lives were saved that day.

Growing up Peter fell in love with the words of the French poet Charles Baudelaire, and he absorbed the works of Hemingway, Charles Bukowski, and Carlos Castaneda. Peter wanted to be an artist like his parents, so just before Peter turned nineteen he moved to Manhattan. His mother had moved to Manhattan at the same age, and she encouraged Peter to move to the big city. It was 1969, and the times were changing. Peter decided to study theater at Hunter College on the Upper East Side. He moved into a cold water flat (no running hot water), a four room apartment on East 76th street between 1st and 2nd. There was a bathtub in the kitchen, and a toilet, but no sink in the bathroom. His roommate was a guy named Phillip who went on to do lab work at MIT Aerospace. The rent was ninety dollars a month.Peter had to work a lot of different jobs during his time in New York City just to pay the bills. He worked in art galleries, waited tables, and even helped build a strip club called Diamond Lills. He built loft beds, painted apartments, and in 1971 Peter got his taxi license, and drove a taxi for eight years. He drove on the weekends, and got familiar with the city. Peter liked working the late shifts. This is when Peter started finding out where to find all the card games in town, and the underground poker tournaments. He knew where you could roll dice for money, where you could bet on ballgames, where to buy any drug you wanted, and where to get a woman any time of the day. Peter could tell you a place that was still serving liquor and steaks at five a.m., if you knew the password. Peter was drinking and partying and doing a lot of cocaine during this time, but this was New York City in the 70s, so everybody was selling and snorting cocaine according to Peter. It was a wild time to be alive in New York City, and Peter knew where to find the action. He always got his cut for taking customers to the action. He wasn't getting rich, but he was living good, and he loved the hustle of life in the concrete jungle.

Peter started a job as a busboy at the Cresthaven Country Club in Whitestone at fourteen. Eventually, he wound up cooking full-time, and started running a few decent joints in Manhattan. He had worked his way up from busboy to head chef by the time he was twenty-five. Peter went on to become a very popular chef, and even won some awards when he worked at Wilson's on the Upper West Side. He also ran two other well known restaurants, Arthur's Court and Bayard's Ale House in the West Village.

Peter loved telling stories about his time as a chef in New York City. One time I asked Peter if he knew Anthony Bourdain. "Terrible chef. Ask anybody in the New York restaurant scene back when Bourdain was around, and they will tell you the truth," Peter said. "The guy was a terrible chef. He blew up after *Kitchen Confidential*, but he couldn't cook to save his life." Peter worked in kitchens in Manhattan around the same time as Bourdain, but he never met him. I didn't tell Peter how big a Bourdain fan I was, and Peter never saw any of Bourdain's tv shows or read *Kitchen Confidential*. "I lived it. Why do I need to read about it?", replied Peter.

Peter loved to cook and continued to cook very well his whole life. I think cooking was like meditation for Peter. It gave him a chance to focus on food, and allowed him a few moments of peace to not think about all the problems in the world, and all the people that needed help. It gave him extreme pleasure to see people enjoying his food.

Peter had started traveling and hitchhiking in high school, and eventually hitchhiked across America several times. After traveling all over the U.S., Peter headed to Europe, and then to Mexico for a few months. Peter fell in love with the Lacandon jungle in Chiapas, Mexico. When he got back to the U.S., the woman he was living with at the time bought him a book called, *Headhunters of the Amazon*, by F.W. Up de Graff. The book was about Up de Graff's time in the Ecuadorian and Peruvian Amazon from 1894-1901. Large sections of the book take place on the Javary River, on the border of Brazil and Peru, a river that Peter would eventually explore. Up de Graff described the Javary as an exotic place, and this really got Peter's attention.

Peter traveled to Iquitos for the first time in 1984, because this was the jumping off point to get the Javary. Peter was accompanied on the trip by a couple of his friends Chuck and Larry, who insisted on going because they feared Peter was going to get himself killed. They flew into Cusco, and hiked the Inca trail to Machu Picchu before flying to Iquitos for a trip to the jungle. They decided against hiring a guide, and decided to take a riverboat twenty hours up the Rio Ucayali to the small jungle town of Requena. They were expecting to find someone to take them out to the jungle. No one would take them anywhere near the jungle.

Peter said there were several dozen people in Requena following them around because they looked so different.

There were not a lot of gringos visiting Requena in 1984, and these gringos stuck out like a sore thumb. The three of them quickly found out that the people of Requena were terrified of the jungle because they believed the jungle had ghosts and bad spirits. They were also terrified of jaguars and the Matses tribe. It had only been fifteen years since the Matses had first made contact with the outside world, and the Matses legends still terrified the people there. Peter, Chuck, and Larry got stuck in Requena for eleven days during the dry season, because very few boats were coming into town due to the low water levels. Finally, they caught a boat back to Iquitos where they hired a guide that Peter had previously turned down. The guide was a short little Peruvian man named Moises Torres Vienna. He was an expert in jungle warfare who had trained U.S. Special Forces in jungle survival. Moises knew the jungle better than anyone and worked as Peter's guide for many years. Moises taught him everything he knew about the jungle. Moises took Peter out in a dugout canoe, and introduced him to ayahuasca for the first time on this trip at the age of thirty-three.

After that trip Peter wrote a story, and submitted the story to *High Times* magazine. After three submissions, *High Times* finally accepted the story, and this would be the first major cover story ever done on ayahuasca. *High Times* had changed editors between his second and third submissions, and their new editor Steve Hagar loved the article. Peter's story, Ayahuasca: Mindbending Drug of the Amazon, made the June 1986 cover of *High Times*. Peter's story helped kick off the ayahuasca tourism boom in Peru.

Peter wrote on 8/4/2009:

But a story in *High Times* magazine, with the cover line, Ayahuasca - Mindbending Drug of the Amazon, as awful as it was, got people's attention. And it was, I later discovered, the first cover story in a national magazine on the topic. As a result of that story, the two big Amazon tour companies operating out of Iquitos at the time began to get requests from their clients to provide this experience to their guests. One of them even sent someone down to talk with one of the curanderos I'd written about - Julio, who became my great friend and teacher - - and asked him if he would come to the Iquitos area once a week and hold an ayahuasca ceremony for tourists. Julio, quite old and a river person who was shy

around outsiders, said no. But Julio's young apprentice, Salis Navarro, said he would do it. And he did. And that was the beginning of ayahuasca tourism. The medicine had always been available to people like me who found ourselves deep in the jungle, but from that point on tour companies found it necessary to offer the medicine as part of their package."

Peter returned to Peru in 1985 to do a month of jungle training with his teacher Moises Torres Vienna. They were on the Aucayacu River when Moises heard about a group of Matses. Moises took Peter, Chuck, and Larry hiking three days into the jungle to set up camp near the Matses. It was only two days later that a young Matses warrior showed up. His face was tattooed with black marks with red achiote painted around his eyes, and long whiskers sticking out from the sides of his nose. The young Matses asked to borrow their shotgun, and Moises handed him two shells. They heard two shots, and a little while later the young Matses warrior showed up carrying two monkeys. Peter's first contact with the Matses had been a success, and he had witnessed a piece of history. After Peter's second trip to Peru, he took several of the Matses artifacts that he had collected to the American Museum of Natural History in New York City. He donated the artifacts to the museum, and those artifacts were put on display in the Museum's Hall of South American Peoples.

Peter went on to write three more freelance stories about Amazonia for *High Times* before they hired him full-time as a Senior Editor. Peter's first investigative story for *High Times* was to get an interview with Dave Foreman, the head of a group called Earth First!, an environmental action group. The problem was that Foreman was on the FBI's most wanted list, and nobody knew where to find him. Peter thought about it for a week, and discovered that Foreman was from Montana or Wyoming. Peter thought that he looked like a big guy from the pictures he saw, so maybe he played high school football. This got Peter to thinking that maybe he liked to have a beer and watch football, so Peter decided to start with Wyoming, and call every bar in the state. It took Peter about two weeks to call information and get the numbers of about two hundred bars in Wyoming. Peter began making calls in alphabetical order. He would start each call, "Hello, this is Peter Gorman, and I'm with *High Times* magazine. I'm trying to reach Dave Foreman of Earth First!, and if you know him can I give you my number for him to call me?" Peter did this for two weeks, and about halfway through the list when he got a call back from Foreman. Peter got the interview, and it was right then that Peter found his calling as an investigative journalist. Peter had been writing most of his adult life, but now he was getting paid to do it as a full-time job.

After Peter went to work full time at *High Times*, he was told by Steve Hager that his number one job was to write about medical marijuana. Peter was one of the first reporters to do stories on hemp. He also wrote several stories on psychedelics like LSD and peyote. Peter held several job titles at *High Times*, and was quickly promoted to Executive Editor. This position meant he got a company credit card, and the power to assign himself interesting stories to write like interviewing Richard Evans Shultes, Dr. Albert Hofmann, Ken Kesey, and Allan Ginsberg.

On his next trip to Peru in 1986 the American Museum of Natural History provided him with a letter from U.S. Customs that stated he was collecting for the museum. And on this trip, Peter took along his brother-in-law Steve Flores. Peter, Steve, and Moises took a small seaplane from Iquitos to Angamos, a small village located on the Rio Javary on the border of Peru and Brazil. At that time Angamos was largely a Peruvian military base, but today it has evolved into a multi- ethnic town with a large presence of Matses culture. Moises rented a boat, and took Peter to Pablo's camp on the Rio Galvez. Pablo was a Matses with four wives and twenty-two children. His camp was called Siete de Junio. The only other adult male at the camp was his brother Alberto, who had two wives and six children.

Peter used the term curacas for the Matses men who had many wives, a quechua word meaning superior or principal, because they were the best at everything they did, and generally the headman of the village. Curacas had to be the best hunters to feed all of the hungry mouths. They had to be the best warriors to keep others from stealing their wives, and they had to be the best medicine men to keep the family healthy. Peter wrote that a good Matses medicine man knows more than a thousand medicinal plants, and he considered his friend Pablo a curaca. Pablo had four wives and almost thirty children to feed. Peter Gorman knew that it was really the women who were in charge because even though the curacas were very powerful; they still had four women who ruled the household. Gorman often mentioned a curaca he knew that was known as Papa Viejo. Papa Viejo had six wives, and was a fierce Matses warrior who fought the Peruvian government up until 1970. He was one of the last holdouts. Papa Viejo was the father of Irene, Peter Gorman's friend.

Moises had known Pablo for a very long time, and Pablo had his wives serve his guests a jungle delicacy, roasted monkey. After dinner Peter would be introduced to the jungle snuff nunu for the first time. Pablo and Alberto took turns blowing the nunu up each other's nostrils through a hollow reed. Then it was Peter's turn, and thus began his thirty-five year love affair with nunu.

Nunu, also known as nene, is a green snuff that is blown up the nasal passages through a hollow reed. Nunu is made from the roasted leaves of nicotiana rustica (tobacco), and the inner bark of wild cacao. The Matses make nunu with two hunters, each one putting their spirit into the hunting medicine. One of the hunters roasts the tobacco leaves over a small fire, and later grounds the leaves into an ash. The other hunter collects the inner bark and cuts the bark into small pieces. The small pieces are placed into a clay pot and cooked long enough so that the pieces can be ground into an ash. The tobacco and the inner bark ash are then placed into a hollow section of bamboo, and pulverized into a powder with a stick. After being pounded into a powder, the nunu is sifted through some type of strainer to remove any remaining large pieces of material. Nunu ends up looking like green flour. If kept dry, nunu can last for years, but the quality of the material lessens over time. Hunters use nunu by pouring the powder into their palm, and then filling up one end of a hollow reed with the powder. The nunu is then blown up the nose of a fellow hunter. The blows are rotated into each nostril several times. Sometimes as many as fifteen in each nostril are received.

Nunu gives hunters focus by providing a grounding, and calming effect. The Matses hunters also use nunu to clear the body, and mind of negative energy. On a physical level, nunu can clear your sinuses of bacteria and mucus. One of the many benefits of receiving nunu is that like sapo it increases your visual acuity, and helps hunters see longer distances with more clear vision, and allows them to identify camouflage animals that they wouldn't normally spot in a normal state of consciousness. Gorman said that the combination of sapo followed by large amounts of nunu is the way that the Matses would traditionally experience these medicines, back-to-back.

Peter told me that when he first met the Matses on the Galvez in the 80s that two hunters would go through a whole bottle of nunu (16-20 oz) in one night before a hunt. Each of them would take turns blowing nunu up the other hunter's nostrils. Dozens of blows would be exchanged. This large amount of nunu they received put them into a psychedelic like state, where spirits would show them visions of where to find animals to hunt. They would have visions of deer, monkeys, anteaters, tapirs, and majas and some of those animals would fall and die in the vision. Those were the animals to hunt, and after the vision the hunters will go to the place they saw in their nunu dream, and wait for the animals to arrive. The Matses believe that the animals see the same vision as the hunters, but the animals only choice is to go meet their maker.

The next morning Pablo introduced Peter to sapo, a frog medicine used by the Matses. Peter was asking Pablo what the Matses called different items when he asked about a leaf bag hanging over the fire. Pablo took down the bag, and pulled out a stick containing the dried secretion of the giant monkey tree frog. He spat on the stick, and used a broken machete to scrape the dried secretion into his saliva, creating a paste he called sapo. Pablo pulled out a piece of vine called tamishi from the bag, and stuck it in the fire to get the end burning red hot. He grabbed Peter by the wrist, burned two dots on the inside of his forearm, and placed the sapo on the dots. Peter became the first non-indigenous person, to have been served sapo, and have his experience published.

When Peter returned to New York, he gave his report to the American Museum of Natural

History. The museum had no record of any tribe in South American using a frog secretion. The problem was that Peter didn't have any proof. He didn't have any photos of the frog or the Matses collecting the secretion or any sticks of sapo. Eventually, Penthouse magazine bought his story about the Matses, but they weren't sure that Peter wasn't making up this story. Penthouse insisted that Peter travel back to Amazonia with their own photographer, Jeff Rotman. So in December of 1986 Peter and Jeff returned to the Galvez with Mosies. They went tapir trapping with Pablo, and captured photographs of the jungle and the Matses. Rotman captured an incredible photo of Peter, Moises, and two Matses men holding a twenty something foot anaconda. Peter brought back several artifacts to the museum, but he could not get a sample of a sapo stick or the frog. Peter still didn't have any real evidence of the frog.

Peter found his way back to Peru in 1988, where he teamed up with Moises for another expedition. But this time, they decided to hike across the jungle from the Rio Tamshiyacu to the Rio Mirin, and from there to the Rio Javary. Moises had a plan to build a raft, and float down the Javary to Leticia, Columbia. It was on this trip that they encountered a small village of Matses about sixty miles from the Matses on the Galvez. Peter exchanged some beads for a stick of sapo. Peter had his holy grail at last. When Peter returned to New York, he gave half the stick of sapo to the American Museum of Natural History, who then gave it to John Daly at the National Institutes of Health. Soon reports started coming out that confirmed Peter's stories about sapo. Vittorio Erspamer, the well-known Italian researcher, sent Peter a letter saying that if it could be shown that the frog was in use by humans, it would be a very important scientific discovery. Peter said, "This would be the first first-hand account in the history of the world - at least according to several scientists, including Mark Plotkin and Richard Evans Schultes - of a human taking an animal substance directly into the bloodstream for medicinal purposes."

Peter was back on the Rio Galvez with his friend Larry in 1990, and Moises helped them find Pablo's new camp in San Juan. Pablo had burned down his old camp because some jaguars had killed a small child. During this visit to the new camp Peter and Larry were the first outsiders to photograph the Matses extracting sapo from the giant monkey tree frog. These were the first photographs that showed the traditional Matses method of having the frog's legs spread out, and tied to four sticks in the ground. This time Peter was also able to take two frogs back with him. He gave one of the frogs to the American Museum of Natural History, and sent the other frog to Erspamer in Rome. In 1993 Erspamer published a paper in the peer-reviewed *Toxicon*, in which he verified everything Peter had said.

Between 1986 and 1993 Peter made several trips on foot from the Ucayali to the Galvez River. Peter also made two additional trips by boat to visit the Matses, and collect plants. These boat trips were partially funded by Shaman Pharmaceuticals, a company that tried to combine ethnobotany with modern medical use. Peter paid to have two boats rebuilt in Iquitos for each trip. The boats were named, the Rey David and the Jacare. Peter hired a team in Iquitos, and went down the Amazon River to Leticia, and then up the Javary River to visit the Matses. Peter and his team ended up collecting over one-hundred plants on their trips to visit the Matses. Peter first met his ex-wife Chepa walking on the boulevard in Iquitos as he was preparing for his second boat expedition in 1993. Chepa's cousin was dating Peter's friend Steve, and her first impression of Peter was that he talked too much, but she found him charming and funny. She was surprised that he was such a big dancer, because he was a gringo.

Peter hired Chepa as part of his crew upon the recommendation of Chepa's brother-in-law Joe

Boatright. Joe Boatright was an oil worker from Coleman, Texas who had married Chepa's sister, and moved to Iquitos after working on oil rigs in Peru. Chepa's father had owned a bunch of riverboats, and was one of the richest men in Iquitos at one time, so she had grown up working on riverboats. Joe knew that Chepa could help keep the boat out of trouble, because she knew the river, and all the military outposts they would be passing through on the way to the Galvez. The military outposts were known for demanding money and goods, and would take whatever they wanted if you didn't have any. The trip with Chepa turned out to be a huge success. The trip lasted thirty-one days, and covered more than fifteen-hundred miles. Peter and Chepa fell madly in love, and less than a year later, they were married.

Peter ended up adopting Chepa's two sons, Italo and Marco, from a previous marriage. They all moved to New York City where Peter worked at *High Times*. After living five years in the big city, Peter and Chepa decided it was time to move the family back to Iquitos along with a new baby girl named Madeleina. The Gormans lived in Iquitos from 1998-2000. Living in Peru allowed Peter to spend a lot more time with his teacher Julio Jerena, and his Matses friends on the Aucayacu, Pepe and Ireni. Peter needed to make some money, so he opened a bar/restaurant on the roughest block in town, right across from the port in Iquitos. The place was called the Cold Beer Blues Bar/ Cevicheria Madeleina. The Cold Beer Blues Bar was the only gringo owned bar in Iquitos at the time. It was a simple bar that mostly served beer, and a few local liquors. The bar played a lot of blues, and a lot of Rolling Stones and Bruce Springsteen. They played local Peruvian music as well, which would lead to dancing in the bar. It was always a party at the Cold Beer Blues Bar. One of Peter's *High Times* softball jerseys hung on the wall, and across the front of the jersey was the name Bonghitters, and this was the first thing customers saw when they walked into the bar. The bar was decorated with lots of jungle artifacts like a fifteen foot black caiman skull that sat in the corner, and a twenty foot anaconda skin that was stretched out above the windows.

Peter described Iquitos as a pretty rough town back then, and Peter had a lot of stories about his bar, and what went on there. Peter believed he had the only joint in town that was anything like a real New York City bar. Located near the port you had to pass through a gauntlet of dock workers carrying twice their weight up steep, muddy slopes all day long. The dock workers were usually high on aguardiente (grain alcohol) that was laced with kerosene and a few hits of pasta base, a by-product of processing raw coca leaf into cocaine. Pasta base is very addictive and more potent than crack cocaine. Fights often broke out near the port, and spilled into the Cold Beer Blues Bar. Peter's regulars included well- intentioned environmentalists, loggers, dope dealers, riverboat captains, spies, and lots of military and mercenary types.

"We were the home of the DEA, the CIA, the Peruvian DEA. We were the home of ex-Pats, the guys who were flying glyphosate over Columbia. We were the home to every rot gut, lousy person in the world here. We had more sins committed in this place than hell knows. It was a wonderful, wonderful bar." said Peter.

Everyone that came into the bar knew that Peter had worked for *High Times*. You couldn't miss the Bonghitters jersey when you walked in the door. They all knew that if they got drunk, and ran off at the mouth that Peter would write about it. Peter at the time was writing a lot for *Narco News*, an online newspaper that covered the drug war. Soldiers of fortune still came to the Cold Beer Blues Bar, got drunk, and spilled the beans on their missions to the bartender/journalist. Peter liked to think he had a hand in shutting down a few operations, and saving innocent lives. One of those stories involved a team of soldiers for hire coming into Iquitos to clear out a section of civilization along the Putomayo River, so they could build a secret army base in Peru to fight rebels in Colombia. The plan was to kill every man, woman, and child who fled into the river as they attacked the rebels, and drove them south from Columbia. One of the mercenaries got drunk and confessed their plan to Peter, who then wrote it up on *Narco News*. Peter got some serious death threats after that mission was canceled.

Shortly after Peter opened the Cold Beer Blues Bar he signed an agreement with a company to take clients on trips out into the jungle for two weeks. The trips went well, and eventually Peter started doing trips that were twenty days long, ten days hiking in Cusco and Machu Picchu, and then ten days in Iquitos, and Amazonia. But in 2006 Peter stopped doing the Cusco portion of the trip after his stomach exploded while he was with clients in Ollantaytambo in the Sacred Valley of Peru. Peter told me when I interviewed him, "I am deathly afraid every time I take a group out to the jungle. I am absolutely terrified that something bad is going to go on and my prayer, a standard prayer, is "Look God if we have to pay a price and something bad has to happen to somebody. Let it come to me cause these people are just on vacation."

Peter and his clients had followed his teacher Victor Estrada to some ruins outside of

Ollantaytambo for a San Pedro ceremony when Peter suddenly got extremely sick. He felt like his stomach was on fire. One of Peter's clients called a doctor who thought it was just gas, but then the doctor called an ambulance when Peter showed no effect after three painkiller shots. The local hospital sent him by ambulance to Cusco. The hospital in Cusco did several tests, and told Peter he was having surgery in two hours. Peter asked for a second opinion, and the doctor told him that if he didn't have surgery in two hours that he would die. The surgery was to treat peritonitis. Peter was saved by a great surgeon in Cuzco. Here's Peter's explanation: "What happened was that I'd gotten an ulcer on my large intestine. I had no idea, no pain, nothing but my big stomach to suggest it. And when I tried to eliminate the old pain, it dug in, and made a couple of holes in that ulcer, which then released three liters of poisoned goup and old stomach acid into my upper body cavity, causing peritonitis."

Twelve days later Peter took a small group of clients out to the jungle, and ripped open his stomach again, and had to have the surgery redone. Peter suffered from a lot of ailments over the years. There were consequences that came with traveling to the exotic places of your childhood dreams. These places were often full of poisonous snakes and spiders, and you're an easy target when you're traveling through impenetrable jungles thick with

with jaguars, and wild dangerous people. Around every corner are things that might kill you, but Peter wasn't scared. Over the years Peter was bitten by many snakes including bushmasters and copperheads. He suffered through a heart attack, and a life threatening case of botfly infestation, and had tough bouts with giardia and malaria. The year before his intestines exploded, Peter had contracted a septic spider bite that opened up large holes in his legs and arms. Peter believed that his fairly regular work with sapo helped him overcome all of these illnesses. He also told me that his access to excellent doctors and hospitals played a big role in keeping him alive after experiencing several serious health conditions throughout his life.

2
QUEENS, TEXAS

All great spirituality is about what we do with our pain
- Richard Rohr

Peter had lived in Texas for a dozen years when I met him. Peter ended up in Texas after his marriage to Chepa ended. Chepa moved to Texas because she had three sisters who had married Texas oilmen working in Peru, and relocated to Fort Worth. Peter wanted to keep his family close, so he left New York City, and found a house in Joshua, about twenty miles south of Fort Worth. Peter knew that bringing a jungle woman not more than four generations removed from deep tribal life to New York City would be a difficult transition. The marriage was not easy, but Peter thought the first five years of their marriage was fantastic. He said that it was all worth it, even with all the fighting and yelling and lots of drinking. Peter once told me a story about how Chepa didn't understand why all the trees were dead when they arrived in the middle of winter in New York City, because they don't have seasons in Amazonia. "If your wife has three sisters, and they live in Lima, well, sooner or later you will live in Lima or the marriage is done. They are the focal point, you are the hunter. You provide, then disappear," Peter said, "It can be loads of fun so long as you know what's coming after the first year or two of marriage."

Peter ended up raising Italo, Marco, and Madeleina as a single dad in that house in Joshua. Peter wasn't cooking in restaurants anymore, but he kept on cooking fine cuisine in his home kitchen. And when Peter wasn't in Peru, he was at home in Joshua being a single dad, and cooking for his three children, and his friends.

Peter wrote on 2/17/2009:

Cooking up a Storm: Well, it's dinner time and I'm just ready to start a nice spaghetti with meat sauce. Or rather, I'm ready to finish the sauce: good garlic and onions, fresh tomatoes, chopped meat cooked separately and strained of most fat, fresh basil, oregano and parsley, good parmesan cooked into the sauce, lots of coarse ground black pepper, a little red wine to keep it loose enough, and then topped with fresh shaved parmesan. Coming with a good mixed greens salad and fresh garlic bread. I've been home about two weeks and when I got here the kids said they missed my

cooking. And with my ankle preventing me from doing much - - it's getting better, thanks - - my normal cooking had to be ratcheted up a notch. Not like we do fancy stuff here as this is not a NYC restaurant and those dishes often take a basic brown sauce just to start - - and that takes 100 pounds of beef bones and 15-20 hours all told - - but we still try to keep it interesting. For breakfast the kids have eaten fried eggs, scrambled eggs, omelets with all sorts of good things, eggs in a nest, French toast, a vegetable souffle. That comes with rice, baked potatoes mashed and fried in a bit of bacon grease, home fries, plantains, tacacho (plantains mashed with bacon grease and bacon bits) and bacon, sliced steak, fried ham wrapped around cheese and so forth. For dinner we've had steaks, roasted chicken with rosemary or done Peruvian style, chicken thighs with vegetarian tomato sauce of fusilli, shrimp sautéed in olive oil and garlic with red peppers, scallions and fresh parsley; mussels posillipo and mussels in white wine; homemade Chinese stir-fry with chicken, chicken burritos with homemade beans, sour cream and rice; bar-be-que with hot links, sweet sausage and chicken, vegetarian lasagna with eggplant, spinach, garlic and three cheeses; lemon chicken (breasts dredged in flour, egg, and breadcrumbs with lots of parmesan, then sauteed and covered with the juice of several great limes), fat hot roast beef sandwiches on good Italian bread with roasted red peppers and pepperjack cheese, and a few things I'm forgetting. Starches have included regular rice, basmati rice, yellow rice, plantains, boiled potatoes with sauerkraut, baked potatoes, mashed potatoes with gravy, potato and egg salad, potatoes au gratin, potato latkes with sour cream, spaghetti squash with red pepper, garlic and sweet onions, homemade macaroni and cheese. Veggies have included steamed broccoli - - almost nightly - - cauliflower, and baby carrot melange with a sprinkling of fresh parsley or cilantro; sauteed spinach with garlic and balsamic vinegar, grilled asparagus, sauteed tomatoes sliced thickly and covered in parmesan cheese, homemade coleslaw, stuffed mushrooms, and so forth. Man, I'm getting hungry. This is good food. About 1/4 of it is organic. And don't forget the breakfast juice: In a blender put a banana, half-pint of fresh strawberries, 2% fat milk, good water, orange juice, and a bit of sugar. Add cantaloupe as you wish. That will wake you up for sure. Just passing it on. Keep the food good, simple, clean and your kids and you will stay healthy. If they were just a little order I could do the rack of lamb en croute persillade with madeira sauce on a wooden

platter surrounded by flaming whiskey mashed potatoes but they're not, so that will have to wait. Whatever you're eating tonight, I hope it's wonderful, makes you healthy and keeps you happy.

In November of 2017 Peter gave me an interview sitting at his kitchen table, and talked about the origin of his mantra:

"So I woke up in that bed, bolt upright and I started singing. Mama Chepa, Mama Chepa. Papa Pedro, Papa Pedro. Italo, Italo. Marko, Marko. Madelaina, Madelaina. Un familia, Me familia. Roto, roto. Broken, broken. My family. I couldn't stop singing it. It went on for two hours. Felt like three years. It went on forever. And then the words came into my head, "more joy, less pain", at the end of that song. It was a beautiful song, like acknowledging that it was a broken family. Acknowledging that we're fucked up. Acknowledging that I'm still Dad, and they're still my kids, and it was hard, and it was horrible. Then "more joy, less pain", and I was like what the fuck are you talking about "more joy, less pain" who the fuck is telling me that? What do I? And it took a couple of days to realize that you're telling me, acknowledge that my family is broken, but that we're still a family, and we still need to function. And every time that Chepa presses a button when she comes over and says 'oh Peter can you go in the bedroom and get me the crotchless panties'. She is not actually going out to fuck somebody in crotchless panties. She's just trying to blow your fucking mind. So instead of responding with, "Watch this, and setting them on fire", remember "more joy, less pain", and with "hun I am not sure where they are, but wow those sound wonderful." So you don't have to give them to her, but she can't respond with pain for you. 'Cause when she says, "you know I might use those with a stranger tonight." The answer is, "he's going to be the luckiest guy." And that produces more joy, because the kids don't hear us arguing. The kids didn't hear me say, "You want the fucking crotchless panties? I'll burn this motherfucker! How dare you!" . . . right . . . which she was really not going to use. If she was going to use 'em, she wouldn't asked me for them. But when you're in the middle of a breakup, you're always thinking you know. You're not realizing she's just being cruel on purpose. And so it wasn't a question of you have to make her turn this way or turn that way. The question was you . . . your job Peter Gorman is to create more joy, and create less pain at every stinkin' turn. No matter how hard that is. When she pushes your buttons, turn around and smile. And when you want to push her buttons, bite your freaking tongue. And you know, even though I failed for six weeks, eight weeks. And I still fail now, twelve years later, now and then. But for the most part our arguments, the animosity ended the minute I stopped responding, and began living with more joy, and less pain."

When Peter had moved to Texas, his employment with High Times ended. Peter had worked his way up all the way to Editor-in-Chief, and spent fourteen years writing for High Times. In 2000 when Gorman was Editor-in- Chief, an Argentine judge demanded his extradition for advocating marijuana use online, a criminal offense at the time in Argentina. While the U.S. refused the request for extradition, Argentina went ahead with the trial and Gorman lost, and he received twenty-two years in absentia.

Peter struggled trying to reinvent himself as a fifty-two year-old freelance journalist in Joshua, Texas. He worked several odd jobs including working as a day laborer to make ends meet. Peter finally landed a steady gig in 2004 when he started writing for the Fort Worth Weekly. Peter lived a quiet family life in Joshua as a single dad, while working as an investigative journalist for the Fort Worth Weekly. He was really devoted to his job as a journalist, and prioritized putting in the necessary time, and effort needed to get the facts right, and the story presented with integrity and accuracy. During his time with the Fort Worth Weekly, Peter won several national awards for stories that he wrote. In 2007 and 2010, the Houston Press Club awarded him 'Print Journalist of the Year' for his work. Peter received a lot of attention for his stories about fracking, and the polluting of the water tables across North Texas during the Barnett Shale fracking boom. The water tables were being poisoned, and making people sick, and no one was writing about it until Peter started making some noise with his stories. Most of his stories were about abuse of power and corruption, and shining a spotlight on those without a voice. He was writing about border detention centers years before the national media picked up on the horror stories that were taking place on the Texas border. Peter's work has been in newspapers like the New York Times, Boston Globe, and several national and international magazines.

Peter continued taking clients to the Amazon after he had moved to Texas, and giving them a taste of what it was like to live in the jungle for a week. Peter promised adventure, magic, and medicine on his trips to Amazonia. Sometimes he would lose five thousand dollars, and sometimes he would make five thousand dollars. He did the trips for over twenty years, and he introduced hundreds of people to life on the Aucayacu, and the teachings of Julio Jerena and his Matses friends.

In May of 2010 Peter released his first book, Ayahausca in My Blood: 25 Years of Medicine Dreaming, with quotes by Dennis McKenna and Dr. Mark Plotkin on the back cover. The book was a huge hit in the plant medicine community, and helped put Peter on the map in the world of plant medicines. In 2013 Peter contracted a flesh eating bacteria when he fell into a pile of fish guts at a market in Jenaro Herrera. Peter told this story on the Hamilton Morris podcast during his last interview before his final Javary expedition. The incident happened late one night when some people had been working negative juju (brujeria) on Peter. Peter was waiting up with three or four of his guests who couldn't sleep, and at five a.m. he really needed to go to the bathroom, but the market was not yet open. Finally when they opened the market bathroom at five-thirty, he raced across the courtyard to relieve himself.

"I wasn't paying attention," Peter said, "And I walked about halfway through what I realized was a puddle of fish guts, and suddenly there was a rope, strung across the thing. It was not a physical rope, but it was an emotional rope that caught me in the neck. My legs went up perfectly flat with my upper body. It was a planche, like if I could have done that in high school I would have won awards for being a gymnast. But it also meant that I was falling down quickly, and as I was falling I thought oh shit, something bad just happened, something really bad. Cause I'm familiar enough with when bad stuff happens. And of course, I landed and banged my head. And I couldn't get out of the fish guts and soap until somebody with a long pole, a twenty foot pole that was used to clean the ceiling, came over and put the pole in there. I grabbed it, and he pulled me out of the fish guts."

Three days later Peter started getting little red streaks of infections on his legs, and it became gangrene. The infection was a flesh eating bacteria combination according to Peter, and it began to eat away at his legs. By the end of the ten day trip, Peter's legs were in terrible shape, and you could see the bone on one of his legs, and they were covered in puss. Peter made it back to the states, and doctors were able to save his legs, because the infection had not made it into the bone. He was lucky that there was really good doctors at the hospital in Burleson who knew how to treat flesh eating bacteria, because these infections were not something that most hospitals treated. The next year Peter was back in Amazonia doing trips. Peter's legs gave him issues the rest of his life, and when he was in Peru they would swell up so bad that he had to wrap them in badges.

Peter published his second book in 2015, Sapo in My Soul: The Matses Frog Medicine. This was the first published book that covered sapo (also known as kambo), and the giant monkey tree frog. Peter started a training course in 2016 for individuals who wanted to be practitioners of the sapo medicine. It was a ten day course that required receiving and serving others sapo every day for ten days. The course was based around Peter's book with lots of additional information about safety when serving sapo. "Sapo is not for everyone and should only be considered on a case by case basis", was one of the ideas taught in Peter's course. I was lucky to witness several of Peter's courses, and you could tell that Peter was happy to be teaching a course that he had designed after thirty plus years of research. Teaching seemed to give validation to the work Peter had been doing. Peter was the frog guru, if there ever was one. Peter only accepted a few people a year for his practitioner courses, and he kept teaching through 2021. It was a tough course, and one that required the right person who could endure the morning and afternoon sapo sessions for ten days in a row. It was a badge of honor to finish the Peter Gorman Sapo School.

Peter released his third and final book, Magic Mushrooms in India: And Other Fantastic Tales in 2021. It's a collection of short stories from Peter's travels around the world from India to Amazonia, and his beloved hometown of New

York City. At the beginning of 2022 Peter prepared to take his third and final expedition up the Rio Javary, almost thirty years after his last expedition to the border of Peru and Brazil. Peter and his team spent a couple of weeks outfitting a boat in Iquitos, and in February with a forty person crew they departed from Iquitos, and sailed down the Amazon River. They spent forty-two days exploring the Javary and Galvez Rivers. Peter was not in the greatest health before he left for the expedition, but he was determined to make the trip. He had surgery on his back a couple of months before he left. His brother Michael was quoted as saying, "He didn't want to waste away at home. He wanted to give the Amazon one last shot." The trip went as planned, and they were able to meet with some of Pablo's family that Peter hadn't seen in thirty years. They visited several Matses villages, and many people remembered Peter from his previous trips. The crew collected a large number of plants, and Peter showed them how to press them.

Peter kept detailed notes of their encounters, and was hoping to turn it into a book about how the Javary had changed over the last thirty years. There were also reports of excessive drinking and infighting on the expedition, but that's not unusual for a forty-two day expedition to remote parts of Amazonia. Peter survived the expedition, but upon his return to

Texas, he fell ill, and was unable to fight off the infections. Peter passed away at the age of seventy-one at a hospital in Burleson, Texas on April 24, 2022.

The tributes poured in after Peter's death, and his death was quite a shock to the world. It was a major loss of an elder in the jungle medicine community. Peter was someone that so many of us relied on for knowledge about jungle medicines. He was the most prominent figure in frog medicine, and the foremost expert in the field for decades. I couldn't count the number of times that I saw Peter mailing out medicine to people, most of the time for free. He always had cat's claw and sacha jergon for people with cancer and tumors. He always had mapachos, and nunu, and a sapo stick if you needed one. Somebody was always sick, and needed Peter's help.

Peter didn't talk a lot about his singing for people every morning, but singing was a big part of his daily ritual. Every morning he would sing for the people who asked him for help. It took me a while to get over the shock of his death, and that he was really gone this time. Peter almost died every year that I knew him, and the older he got, the harder it was for his body to recover. Peter had been through a lot in his seventy-one years. I guess I always knew the day was coming, but I never expected the void to be so large.

I am grateful for the time I spent at his house working on the documentary. I miss listening to his jungle stories, and all the incredible food that he cooked, and I'll never forget those suppers watching *The Rockford Files* with him and Madeleina. Peter was an open book, and a fantastic subject for a documentary. All you had to do was put the camera on him, and Peter would take over. He was a natural storyteller, and I always thought that he would have been a terrific actor. Storytelling was in his blood. Peter had abilities that I still can't explain. Peter knew things, and was a rock in my life when I needed it.

Peter wrote on 3/24/2007:

But here's the thing: The Matses, and other indigenous groups have been so generous in sharing their secrets that I don't think I've really done anything except listen to them and take them seriously. If they say I should follow them into the woods, I do, without hesitation. There they show me the anaconda; or a group of large white collared peccary or fantastic plant medicines. And over the years I've done everything they've asked of me but for three things. One of those is to follow the fossil bed--which is located at the mouth of a creek that can only be seen in extreme low water season--to its source. Another is to follow the Yakirana all

the way up into the Andes Mountains, which is where the Matses say they came from; the third is to explore some pyramid shapes in the jungle that they tell me are very important.

Terence McKenna in 1991: Tree frog from Peru. This is all Peter Gorman's fieldwork, and I respect Peter Gorman. He's not a personal friend of mine, because I haven't spent that much time with him, but he seems to know about this than anybody else. He's the only white person to have any information first hand about it. His account is that these extremely uncontacted people in the Amazon have a tree frog which exudes something on its belly, and they take a burning stick, and burn a whole in the muscle of the upper arm, just like you would take a cigarette and burn a hole into your arm. Then they pack this hole with this material from the underbelly of this frog, and then a spectacular trip results. This is entirely the reports of one fieldworker, which is a dream come true for him. This is what we all want to do, is to go off and find a powerful hallucinogen that nobody else knows anything about, and bring it back.

Dennis McKenna: Peter was a colorful character and a wild adventurer who was widely beloved. His heart was in the Amazon, and he introduced many people to its wonders and it's medicines over many years as a guide and explorer: I fondly remember the several occasions we ran into each other when we were passing through Iquitos back in the day. We often shared cervezas (beers) and mapachos (strong Amazonian tobacco) while hanging out on the Malecon (promenade on the waterfront), watching the world go by and pondering the mysteries of life. There will be never be another Peter Gorman. He will be missed.

Chris Kilham: Peter Gorman and I first met in Iquitos around 2007, and we struck up a friendship. Often, when I was there, he would be coming or going for one of his jungle ayahuasca tours, and I would be heading in or out with the Ayahuasca Test Pilots. Peter would sit in front of the restaurant La Masion nursing a beer, and he would tell stories and opine about any number of things for as long as I was willing to sit with him. We exchanged books we had written, and swapped quotes for new books. Peter was smart, insightful, a bit jaundiced, and funny. He seemed to operate with little regard for his personal safety, and thus got hurt a lot. I enjoyed him immensely. Peter got to the Amazon earlier than almost all of us, and he went deep in, with ayahuasca, sapo and more. He deserved his legend and had the dings and snake bites to prove his jungle cred. He was bold and very much one of a kind. I will miss Peter, miss seeing him on the Iquitos Promenade, and miss his yarns and laugh. He made a great contribution to the psychedelic scene.

Mark Plotkin: Peter Gorman was an ethnobotanical Ernest Hemingway. His travels were equally adventurous, and his writing was equally insightful and hard knuckled. Whereas Hemingway's drugs of choice were absinthe and rum, Peter preferred ayahuasca and kambo (sapo). His books on both of those mind-altering substances are classics. Although he was, at heart an Amazonian, quotes from two Europeans my best sum up him and the way he lived: in Alfred Tennyson's Ulysses, the narrator says "I will drink life to the lees," and in Rafael Sabatini's Scaramouche, the protagonist is described thus: "He was born with a gift of laughter and a sense that the world was mad.

Morgan Maher: Father, brother, friend, guide, explorer, writer, journalist, playwright, chef, restauranteur, cabbie, confidant, raconteur, medicine man, jefe de jefes, the one, the only, the modest, the magical, the mighty — Peter Gorman. Every time I think of him, look at him and his life, he keeps getting bigger, taller, higher, wider, deeper, and stronger. I met Peter in Iquitos in 2007 when, on a whim, I joined one of his jungle jaunts, and we remained close friends ever since. Well known for his work with Amazonian shamanism, Peter's life story is as unique and bedazzling a place as the jungle. An old school New Yorker, Peter helped build Jimmy Hendrix's Electric Ladyland, smoked ganja with Bob Marley while building the Island Records studio, was an occasional assistant to the artists Robert Rauschenberg and Claes Oldenburg, was "the guy who pulled the squeegee across the silk screens for Warhol's Marilyn's, Mao's and Flowers" and stamped Warhol's signature, he wrote four off-Broadway plays, ran several successful restaurants, and was the editor of High Times magazine. And that's just a few bits I recall from stories told with a gravelly New York accent, Irish eyes, journalistic detail and theatrical flair. Peter was once described as the "real life Indiana Jones", and into that pot you could surely stir a kind of psychedelic, counterculture Forrest Gump. He just seemed to pop up in a long list of culturally significant moments. Eventually Peter fell in love with the Amazon and poured his rich and storied life into the jungle, while it's rivers, peoples, forests and medicines poured into him. And he brought others along on this wild, extraordinary adventure — deep into the jungle and the magical world. Others who became guests, guests who became friends, friends who became family. It is impossible to quantify or overstate the direct impact, influence and inspiration Peter had on hundreds, probably thousands of people. And that energy, force and magic Peter cooked up and shared so generously — carries on exponentially.

Peter Gorman was one of the most interesting guys that I have ever known. Peter was always right on the edge of being a huge star. "Who the hell is Peter Gorman?" was a phrase that I heard Peter use several times when I discussed the documentary with him. His legacy, and what he had done in his life was important to him. Below is an email Peter sent me after watching a rough cut of the film. I still laugh every time I read it, because as usual Peter was right on the money:

I was wondering if in the beginning of your movie if you have a voice over where you explain who Peter Gorman is, what he's done, how you met him, and the effect he has had on your life? If you do, fantastic. If not, it might be something you might consider to get people into why they are going to be watching this movie. And if I'm just stupid and missed it, forgive me. - Peter G

Peter Gorman's 2015 interview with Tom Huckabee:

Peter Gorman: One of my greatest joys. The day I knew I made it. Now tell me the name of *Even Cowgirls Get the Blues*.

Tom Huckabee: Tom Robbins.

Peter Gorman: I'm at home, before I met Chepa, and I'm living alone on East 90th Street, and I get a phone call, and the phone call says, 'Hello, this is Tom Robbins. I hope I'm not bothering you.' I said Tom Robbins, I-- 'The Author Tom Robbins. I've written a couple of books.' Oh Tom Robbins, Jesus! Yeah cool, you calling me, what for? 'I hope you don't mind. Terence gave me your number.' And I said, hold on, and before he said one more word, I was like yes, yes Terence gave Tom Robbins my number. And I said what do you want, and he said it turns out that you're the one that knows everything about this frog, and I'm writing a book called *Half Asleep in Frog's Pajamas*, and I need to talk to you about the frog, because I don't know anything about it. Of course, it turned out that he was not talking about my frog, sapo. Now known often as kambo. My new book is about that. But he was talking about the bufo alvarius toads. So in the end, I didn't have a ton of information to give him, you know, so the phone call didn't work, but the fact that Terence McKenna had me in his phone book to pass on to Tom Robbins to call me was, made me feel like yes, I really am a writer. Somebody knows me, and that was just one of the highlights of my writing career.

Peter Gorman's 1995 Interview with Richard Shultes:

Often called the Father of modern ethnobotany, botanist, explorer and author Richard Schultes is the Director Emeritus of Harvard's famed Botanical Museum. Beginning in 1940, Dr. Schultes spent a total of 17 years in the Amazon, mostly in the remote regions of Colombia where he investigated and collected the medicinal, edible and toxic plants used by the Kofan, Witoto and other indigenous groups. He is the recipient of dozens of awards for his pioneering botanical work, among them the Cross of Boyaca—Colombia's highest honor—and The Gold Medal of the World Wildlife Fund, presented by Britian's Prince Philip. Additionally, he has authored and co-authored numerous books—including two written with LSD synthesizer Dr. Albert Hofmann—among them Plants of the Gods—Origins of Hallucinogenic Use (Schultes and Hofmann; 1979, McGraw-Hill, NY) and The Healing Forest: Medicinal and Toxic Plants of Northwest Amazonia (Schultes and Raffauf; 1990, Dioscorides Press; Portland, OR). Now 80 years old, Dr. Schultes, the father of three grown children, continues to work at the Botanical Museum two days a week, is concentrating on finishing several book projects, and is hoping to make one more trip to his beloved Colombian Amazon.

PETER GORMAN: Let's start with how you came to be an ethnobotanist.

RICHARD SCHULTES: Well, I'm from an old New England family, and when I was growing up one of my uncles had a farm up in what was then a small town, Townsend, Massachusetts. I spent the summers up there, helping in the haying, and I began to collect plants. I don't know where I learned that you pressed them, but I pressed them in big encyclopedias. Then I began to learn what the vernacular names of the plants were and as I got older I learned that they had Latin names—which didn't mean much to me until I studied Latin. So I always had an interest in plants.

PG: What did you study in school?

RS: Well, I did my undergraduate thesis on peyote. I went out to Oklahoma with an anthropologist, Weston LaBarre—who was then a graduate student at Yale and later became famous writing several books on peyote—and attended four or five all night ceremonies and tried peyote with the Indians. We spent time with three or four different tribes, mainly Kiowa. Anyway, I collected some peyotes and brought them back and did a little chemical work on it.

PG: Were you the first to do chemistry on the peyote cactus?

RS: No. But I'd had several courses in organic chemistry and I just became interested in it. I'm ashamed of it now because it's very complicated and I was just a beginner at chemistry. But in writing my thesis I became interested in a misconception that had taken hold in relation to peyote and the sacred plant of the Aztecs, Teonanacatl. William Safford, an ethnobotanist—I think he was with the Smithsonian—had said in 1916 that the Aztec's Teonanacatl must have been peyote. Which did not fit in with my knowledge of botany because peyote is a cactus and cacti do not grow in high wet forests, while Teonanacatl was undoubtedly a fungus, a mushroom which doesn't grow in deserts. And so I went to Mexico hoping I'd be able to see this plant, Teonanacatl, and I ended up doing my thesis on the useful of plants of the Mazatec Indians.

PG: Did you ever find Teonanacatl?

RS: Yes. I was able to bring back one identifiable species of this mushroom they were using, Panaeolis sphinctrinus, and in 1941 I published a paper in the Harvard Botanical Museum Leaflets identifying that one species as Teonanacatl. Of course, thanks primarily to the work of Gordon Wasson and the Mexican mycologist Gaston Guzman, we have since learned there are about twenty-four species used by the Shamans of Oaxaca.

PG: Did you get to do the magic mushroom with the Mazatec's?

RS: No. I hadn't tried it. I only had a couple of specimens. But I fell in love with Oaxaca and thought I'd probably work all my life there on the flora.

PG: What changed your mind about continuing to work in Mexico?

RS: Well, after I'd gotten my PhD, I had two jobs offered to me: biology master in a private school in New England and a grant from the National Academy of Sciences to go to the Amazon to find out what plants the natives used in making their curare.

PG: Why was the National Academy of Sciences interested in curare?

RS: Because in late 1930s, scientists had isolated a chemical from one of the plants used to make curare called tubocurine, which was just becoming very important in medicine. It's a muscle relaxant that's now used in any good hospital before deep surgery. Now the Indians make many different kinds of arrow poisons so the Academy wanted to know as much as possible about the different plants they used. So that was the job I took. I took a plane down to Bogota in 1940 and worked out in the field on that project.

PG: How did you first go into the jungle?

RS: I first went in with Indians who lived along the base of the Andes mountains in Colombia, some of whom spoke Spanish. So I had an entree. And as I went farther inland I got Spanish speaking Indian boys who spoke the language of one or two of the tribes and that way I got in among them. But they certainly knew I was there before I did, because the grapevine from one tribe to another is much more efficient than Western Union. So even some of the people who hadn't had any contact with outsiders knew I was in the area and what I was doing. I spent a lot of time with the Witotos. I did quite a bit of work with them and also with the Kofan, both of whom make a number of arrow poisons from different plants. Later when I heard about the outbreak of World War ll I thought I would be conscripted, so I made my way back to Bogota and went to the US Embassy there. But instead of conscripting me they told me to go back into the jungle and try to stimulate the production of rubber. This Bostonian who'd never cut a rubber tree, but I'd been with the Indians nine months at that time so they assumed I had learned all about that.

PG: And how did you do?

RS: Well, I gathered a lot of material from species that had been known from the last century, and I also discovered one new species of dwarf rubber tree. It's an endemic species, only found on one mountain in the Amazon, a mountain that has many unique plants on it. It's recently been made a protected biological area. This is the mountain that's been named for me.

PG: I didn't know there was a mountain that had been named for you. What's it called?

RS: Mesa Schultes. Mesa means table. So it's Shultes' Table. Before that I had a cockroach I collected in the Amazon named for me, and I thought that was a great honor. It's the genus called Shultesia. But I've come up from cockroaches to mountains.

PG: There are a number of plants with your name as well, aren't there?

RS: Oh, yes, about two hundred and ten species. Plants are frequently named for the collector. A number of my plants are also named for the Indians who use them. That's also very common among botanists, to use geographical or tribal names.

PG: What's the process of collecting a plant?

RS: The first thing you do is take a cutting of the plant and press it between sheets of newspaper in a plant press so that you can identify it later. Fruits and flowers are very helpful here, we always try to get them. Without this, what we call the herbarium specimen, you have nothing. The second thing you do, if you want to later analyze the plant's chemicals, is to take a wide mouthed plastic jug and put some 70 percent ethyl alcohol into it and then cut the plant in half-inch pieces and put the pieces into the alcohol. The alcohol—provided you use ethyl, and not methyl or booze—will not change the chemical composition of the substances. If they are leached out, they will be in the alcohol which the chemist will have. Actually it's much more easily worked with that way than if the chemicals are in the actual plant material. That's the only way to collect.

PG: And how did the Indians feel about your collecting their plants?

RS: The Indians are wonderful natural collaborators, because they are so interested and knowledgeable about their flora. Everyone was always interested in why I wanted this plant or that plant. The fact was, I wanted it because they used it. If they asked me why I wanted something, I made up a disease we use it for—I've invented more diseases than we ever had, so they think we're a good deal more decrepit than we actually are.

And then they'd often say "You can't use that plant for that. That plant is for treating earaches," or something like that. That's how I'd find out how they used it, you see?

PG: How many medicines have been made from the plants that you've taken?

RS: Very few. There's one that's called yoco which has a very high content of caffeine which is now used to reduce obesity. I also have a couple of things in Sweden that are being looked at, and several that the American company Shaman Pharmaceuticals are looking into. But American companies, until recently, have looked down their noses at plant chemistry. They have no interest in it. I'm glad some of them are starting to take notice because when you consider that the Amazon has 80,000 species of higher plants—and Indonesia, Southeast Asia, or Africa have at least that many as well—well, this is a tremendous chemical storehouse.

PG: Did you ever need an indigenous medicinal remedy?

RS: No. I really never got sick in the Amazon except for malaria and I always had chloroquine for that. It was always the first thing I put in my briefcase. It's generally very healthy there. There's tuberculosis and leprosy, which is very common, but that can be controlled if you have soap with you.

PG: There's an African shrub called Iboga plant, which is used, among other things, to stop people from obsessive behavior. It's currently being looked into by the National Institute of Drug Abuse as an addiction interrupter. I've heard stories that ayahuasca is sometimes used similarly to treat alcoholism. Have you heard that as well?

RS: No, I haven't, but I'm convinced that some of these so- called drugs will have side effects that can be used in certain diseases or conditions. For example, one of the big problems that exist among American Indian tribes is that so many of the young people become alcoholics. Many of these people stop drinking when they go to these peyote ceremonies, and I'm sure its not only religious teachings in the ceremonies, but the weekly taking of peyote that's helping them as well. But most of these things have not been properly looked at by medically oriented people. Some of the chemicals in them have not been investigated at all. And chemists take the chemicals that we get out of these compounds and change them to make semi-synthetic compounds. The possibility of making something that may have a special effect is enormous. That's what I think when I see these forests burning up or being cut down in Brazil. It's a crime against humanity. One of the best Brazilian botonists has written that he calculates less than one percent of the Amazonian flora of Brazil has been even superficially looked at by chemists.

And so imagine what we are destroying in the Amazon alone! Thousands of species that we'll never be able to analyze and many of them we don't yet even have botanical names for.

PG: What can be done to save this knowledge of the people's whose native regions we're so quickly destroying?

RS: Civilization, our culture, is advancing with every road, every airport, every commercial company after wood. And with missionaries, tourists and others who are coming into contact with primitive peoples and, while not purposely maybe, certainly destroying their cultures. This is one of the things I've argued for: ethnological conservation. We've got to preserve the knowledge of these peoples. For example, one of my former students and best field men, Dr. Michael Ballick, is taking as much time as he can from his job at the Botanical Gardens in New York to work in

Belize where there are three or four old medicine men; if they die all the knowledge of what they're using is gone. He has a woman there who speaks their language who works with these medicine men and he goes down three or four times a year and she gives him the notes. It's a wonderful thing. All that will be saved.

PG: Once we've saved their knowledge, how do we make sure that the indigenous people from whom it comes get their fair share?

RS: There's a lot of discussion about that and many drug companies have agreed to see that some help, whether its financial or some other way, gets back to the tribe. Where I worked, money would be useless, absolutely useless. They don't need money. It would have been much better for me if they had since I had to pay them in things and had to carry all the stuff down into the jungle. But in many other places where they can use money, money can be given to the tribe or some representative of the tribe. In the case of Shaman Pharmaceuticals, they have set up a special sub-branch of environmental conservation, The Healing Forest Conservancy. And they've agreed that if they make any money from any of the things they get from the Indians, that they will give back to the group in some way or another. Either by sending a doctor there, or sending money if they can use it, or sending a bright young boy out and giving him a year or two in school somewhere. There are many ways of doing this.

PG: And how do we save the environments of these peoples?

RS: This is another thing I argue for: botanical and environmental conservation. In many places, especially in Brazil, commercial interests are bringing in all sorts of mechanical material and cutting not only the trees they want, but taking down every twig. The pictures that you see from Brazil are horrendous. I've seen them cutting everything down and letting it dry and then setting it afire, and then, of course, nothing else grows. What we'll have is a great extension larger than the United States, of desert scrub, small plants and trees. You'll never get the forest taking over.

PG: Is the same true in Colombia?

RS: No. Thanks to the lack of much white penetration and thanks to the rapids and the rivers which make navigation with boats impossible on all but the Putumayo River, the destruction is only by Indians with axes. They cut enough to get their food, period. They don't take down a thousand acres at a time. They work those clearings for five or eight years until the land doesn't give any more crops, and then they move. And in those small areas the jungle takes back over. Which it doesn't when you cut large areas.

PG: Isn't a large part of the problem population explosion, particularly in the 3rd World?

RS: I have long thought that the number one crisis facing the world is population. For every child born it means a few inches less soil for food. And the way we're destroying the forests and agricultural land, we no longer have the luxury to procreate the way we have. You have to make people aware, particularly in a place like Colombia, that after two or three children they have to stop. Now the Colombian government was doing this with medical advice, and then the Pope comes in there, the first stop of any Pope in the New World—and Colombia is a very Catholic country—and he berates the government for this. He should stay over in Rome and leave governments alone. But he said this was a terrible thing to do and most of the ordinary Colombian people, being so strongly Catholic, believed him. Fortunately the government didn't. They're still doing it.

PG: Let me ask about your vision plant experiences. Tell me about using ayahuasca and virola snuffs with the indigenous people. You must have had some extraoradinary experiences…

RS: I wouldn't call them extraordinary. With virola snuff you don't usually have same effects that you get with ayahuasca. I have taken peyote in ceremonies with the Indians, and ayahuasca, and with both of these I get color reactions. But I never had visions and I don't see things, although I know that many people do. With peyote, for example, or mescaline, many people see things from our culture. And the Indians, with ayahuasca, see huge snakes and jaguars and in some cases, if they have been indoctrinated to think they can, they see other-world spirits, or the spirits of their ancestors. But I have never seen anything except color. If you remember Walt Disney's Fantasia, the first thing is a color interpretation of Bach's Tocata and Fugue.

That's the closest I can tell you of my experience with peyote and with ayahuasca. I see vague things like clouds or smoke of different colors going across my field of vision, but I've never seen anything concrete. I think this is mostly a psychological difference; that these people expect to see those things. As a scientist, I don't expect to see them.

PG: You've had a long relationship with Dr. Albert Hofmann. How did you two meet?

RS: I met him in a conference in Berlin. I knew that he was interested in the work of Mr. Wasson on the intoxicating mushrooms. That was when Wasson was just beginning that work. So I said I'd been in the Oaxaca area and knew a little about them. And that struck up a friendship. We boycotted a lot of lectures and just sat and talked. And after that we wrote two books together. We're great friends.

PG: Did you ever do Hofmann's LSD?

RS: No. I always told him I didn't want to because it wasn't a natural thing, it was a synthetic. And because of that I had no interest in it.

PG: What about Gordon Wasson, the mycologist?

RS: Well, I went to the Amazon right after Mexico and I hadn't been home for two years during the war—I was getting rubber out—and when I finally got home this banker called up from New York and said "I know of your paper in which you identified one species of mushroom as Teonanacatl. I'm going to go down there because this is very interesting to me. Can you give me some names?" Well, I didn't know anything about Wasson, and I told him it had been several years since I was last in Mexico but gave him the name of a doctor, Dr. Reko, who worked in Oaxaca and who'd been interested in these mushrooms too. So Wasson went down to Mexico and got in touch with this doctor who set him up with names of people to see.

PG: Wasson and yourself later became good friends, didn't you?

RS: We became very close friends. He even had an honorary appointment in the Harvard Botanical Museum, because even though as far as science goes he was an amateur—in the best sense of the word, a lover of knowledge—he was doing research that no one else had done. And publishing it. He published I think six or seven books in the 22 years he had an honorary appointment.

PG: Did you ever get to use the mushrooms?

RS: No. Because I never went back to Mexico. I would have had I been with Wasson on one of his trips, as Albert Hofmann was.

PG: Is there any truth to the stories that Wasson kept them around for his guests….

RS: I don't think that's true. He gave most of his specimens to the museum here. You can see them in our lecture hall in bottles.

PG: What about datura? Is that something you've used?

RS: There are six species in the Andes of South America, and a number of the Indians do use it, alone or with other hallucinogens. But I would never take a solanaceous plant.

PG: Why not?

RS: The scopolomine and atropine which they contain are very very toxic alkaloids. And not only that, the concentration of these alkaloids in a single plant can vary from one season to the next and very often from one day to the next. In any event it's too dangerous to fool with. I wouldn't do it.

PG: What are your feelings about drug use in our society?

RS: I am concerned with the excessive use of drugs like marijuana and cocaine, but I don't know what you can do about it, especially cocaine. Coca, you know, is harmless when used by the Indians, who chew the leaves of the coca bush. But that's quite different than processed cocaine. I'm sorry about what

Columbia is going through now, with their drug problems. But who's responsible? We are. If we didn't buy the cocaine or Europe…well now Japan is buying it. They're having a terrible problem there.

PG: I'm not a fan of cocaine either. Marijuana, you and I might disagree on…

RS: I don't necessarily disagree with you on that, except I think it's got to be controlled in a motorized civilization. The effects of marijuana differ with different people and at different times with the same person. But there are two things it always does, and in the beginning when you don't feel too woozy you don't recognize them: It distorts the sense of time and of space, both of which you absolutely need when you're driving. But I do think they should decriminalize it. I have been to court many times to testify for these young kids who were caught sharing a marijuana cigarette with a friend and they want to put them in jail and make a real criminal out of them. What a travesty of justice.

PG: You've joked about being the guru for the psychedelic generation. Did you and Wasson and Hofmann ever sit around and laugh about being the trinity of psychedelia?

RS: Well, yes. We were all in a meeting some years ago which Jonathan Ott put on in San Francisco, and he had all sorts of experts on hallucinogenic plants there. The peyote man, Weston LaBarre was there, and Albert Hofmann and myself and Wasson and many other people. And we naturally thought it was funny, all of us there in our suits and ties, not looking like gurus at all. Well, I'm not a guru and never thought about myself that way. I used to lecture down there in California during the hippie days, and I think many people were disappointed when they saw me. They thought I would look like Allen Ginsberg or something.

PG: Despite your conservative appearance you really did usher in the psychedelic revolution, the three of you. Shultes, Hofmann, and Wasson…

RS: I don't think I did, but altogether I suppose you could say we did. Actually, I think Mr. Leary did more than any one of us in ushering in that.

PG: Do you regret your part in bringing the idea of vision drugs to the Western world?

RS: No. I don't. Not at all. I never have.

3
Frog Magic

If it's your job to eat a frog, it's best to do it first thing in the morning. And if it's your job to eat two frogs, it's best to eat the biggest one first.
- Mark Twain

Frogs have always played an important role in our culture, and people throughout time have used frogs for a variety of purposes such as amulets, fertility medicine, poison, and magical potions. Frogs are featured in art, haikus, legends, movies, myths, plays, poems, proverbs, and songs. Stories about frogs can be found in religious texts worldwide, and in certain cultures, frogs are linked with themes of cleansing and rebirth. This might have to do with the life cycle of a frog, and it's transformation from an egg to a tadpole, and into an adult amphibian. Artwork and statues found in ancient cultures shows us that frogs were an important part of life. The Chinese used a frog poison in the 17th century to make explosives, and the use of frogs in Europe dates back to the 13th century.

In ancient Egypt frogs symbolized life and

fertility, and in Egyptian mythology there was even a frog goddess known as Heqet. Some researchers believe that the Eqyptian frog symbolism was related to the annual flooding of the Nile River from which millions of frogs were born. The annual flooding meant rich soil and strong crops, so when there was millions of frogs, this would lead to a good planting season. Many ancient Egyptians believed that if you wanted to conceive that you should touch a frog. The Greeks and the Romans also associated frogs with fertility and harmony. In many Chinese tales, frogs were the keeper of powerful secrets of the world, including the secrets of immortality. In Japan, frogs are considered symbols of good luck. The Irish believe that you can tell the weather by the color of a frog. A dark colored frog was a sign of rain, while a light brown or yellow frog meant dry weather.

Frogs have long held diverse significance in Native American culture, with many tribes across North America believing in their healing powers and their ability to bring rain. Frogs have been featured in the works of Shakespeare and Mark Twain, while modern times have introduced iconic frog characters like Kermit the Frog.

Frogs are bioindicators of a healthy ecosystem. They play essential roles in the food chain, both as the predator, and the prey. When frogs are in their tadpole stage, they consume algae, which plays a crucial role in reducing algae contamination in waterways. This natural process helps maintain clean waterways, and contributes to filtering our drinking water. When frogs are grown they eat insects such as mosquitoes, and flies. Without frogs, insect populations flourish, leading to the spread of more diseases like, dengue, malaria, and west nile. Frogs also provide a food source for birds, fish, monkeys, and snakes. Frogs have a major influence on the populations of other species in an ecosystem, and a disappearance of frogs can have major effects on the entire ecosystem.

Many indigenous tribes in South America are known to have worked with the secretion of the giant monkey tree frog including the Amahuaca, Cashinahua, Cocama, Katukina, Kaxinawa, Kulina, Matses, Marubo, and Yawanawa. There are several others who claim to use it as well. In 1925 the first reported use of the giant monkey tree frog secretion was documented by a French missionary, Constantin Tastevin, who was staying with tribes in Brazil. In 1969 Explorer Loren McIntyre witnessed a frog medicine ritual with the Matses along the Brazil/Peru border. Peter Gorman's report of his sapo experiences got out in 1986. And today you will find a frog medicine practitioner in almost every major metropolitan area in the world. Word about the giant monkey tree frog has spread fast. There are various perspectives on this development, but the undeniable power of this frog medicine is evident in the compelling results that it has produced.

The giant monkey tree frog is scientifically classified as the phyllomedusa bicolor, and is known by many names such as giant leaf frog, giant waxy tree frog, and others depending on where you are in Amazonia. The Matses tribe refer to the frog as acate. In this book I refer to the phyllomedusa bicolor as the giant monkey tree frog, which is found in several countries across South America including eastern Peru, northern Brazil, southeastern Columbia, and parts of Boliva, Ecuador, French Guiana, Guyana, Suriname, and Venezuela. The giant monkey tree frog is bright green on its back and legs, with a black/white/yellow underbelly, and has long legs and toes. These frogs are nocturnal. The males are arboreal spending most of their lives living high up in the trees, while the females spend most of their lives swimming in rivers and streams, and laying near ponds of water.

The giant monkey tree frog is a large frog compared to most frogs found in Amazonia, but it's still small enough to fit in the palm of your hand. The males are 3.5 - 4 inches in length while the females are slightly larger at 4 - 4.5 inches. The lifespan of the giant monkey tree frog in captivity is ten years, but it is not known what the life expectancy is in the wild. They reproduce throughout the year, but the height of their breeding season occurs during the wet season in South America, which is November to May. They lay as many as six hundred eggs at a time near streams. Ten days after the eggs are laid, little tadpoles hatch from their shells, and make their way into the water. The eggs of the giant monkey tree frog are heavily targeted by predators such as snakes.

The giant monkey tree frog has a very distinct mating call: "bak, bak, bak." They perform their mating calls at night, and the bak calls can be heard from a long distance away. The beautiful call of the giant monkey tree frog is unmistakable. These frogs reproduce through amplexus, which is a position where the male grabs the female from behind, and fertilizes the eggs. This positioning can last up to two days. This kind of commitment is not common in the animal kingdom. The competition to find females can be fierce, and according to a report that came out in 2010, the males push other males off of females during amplexus. They use their heads to shove rivals, and sometimes their hind legs, as well as a series of aggressive calls and antics.

The secretion produced by the giant monkey tree frog also acts as a defense mechanism against predators. If an anaconda tries to swallow the frog, it will secrete this solution, and the snake will be forced to release the frog. The giant monkey tree frog has fewer predators in the jungle than most amphibians. Their biggest threats come from humanity, and the commitment to the deforestation and development of Amazonia. Studies have found that this secretion is also a part of the frog's immune defenses against fungal and microbial infections. Researchers consider this part of the reason why the giant monkey tree frog populations seems to be growing while other amphibian species are dwindling in numbers because of climate change and diseases.

These days the Matses on the Aucayacu River venture out at night in motorized canoes to locate the giant monkey tree frogs high up in the trees overlooking the river. The Matses mimic the frog's mating call to elicit a response from a frog, helping pinpoint the location of the frog. They use battery powered headlamps to spot the frogs, and a collector will then climb up the tree to retrieve the frog. The trees are usually fifty to eighty feet tall. It takes a lot of bravery, and skill to climb those towering trees at night over snake infested waters. Climbing eighty feet up a tree at night without a rope seems crazy in Western society, but to the Matses, it's just a normal part of daily life. After finding the frog, they will cut off the tree branch that the frog is sitting on, and take down the branch with the frog on it. They don't want to disturb or touch the frog too much. The Matses believe it is crucial to minimize physical contact with the frog before extracting the secretion from it. They believe that it is best to keep the frog as calm as possible, and not adding any additional stress on the frog. They do not want to anger the frog spirits.

After the frog is brought back to camp, the Matses cut four small sticks around eighteen inches long, and stake them into the ground in a rectangular pattern. Each of the frog's legs are carefully secured to the four sticks using pieces of vine. Once the frog has been secured to the sticks, a small wooden stick is stuck up the frog's nose to make it slightly uncomfortable, so it will discharge a secretion on its outer skin. The secretion is dispersed mainly on the frog's back and outer legs. The Matses use a flat wooden stick to scrape the secretion off the frog, and place the secretion on a type of hardwood that does not absorb the secretion. Traditionally they will not milk the frog completely dry of its secretion, and this allows the frog to keep some of its natural defense mechanism.

I have read where some practitioners call this traditional collection method a "crucifixion", and advertising that they only sell "non-crucified medicine". Having seen and filmed the Matses way of medicine collection, I can honestly say that this is not an accurate depiction. There may be individuals out there who are harming the frog when collecting medicine, but the traditional Matses method does not harm the frog. It's definitely not a crucifixion, because the frog is immediately released back into the jungle after the collection. And traditionally the Matses would not want to anger the animal spirits. This exchange between the Matses and the frog is a beautiful balance of humans and wildlife living in harmony together. The secretion creates value for the frog's life, and keeps it from being roasted over the campfire like most animals in the jungle. Other tribes hold the frog, and collect the secretion by tapping the frog on the head with a stick.

When the secretion dries on the hardwood, it looks like a clear translucent material. You might best describe the dried secretion as looking like clear coat varnish. You can tell a Matses stick from other collectors, because their sticks are beautifully layered across the stick shining crystal clear like a piece of glass. Most of the Matses sticks are about a foot long with one end carved in a v-shape. The v-shape is the end they hold when scraping off the secretion. They scrap the sapo off the stick using any instrument that has a sharp edge. I've seen everything from broken machetes to butter knives used. I've seen people use Swiss Army knives, and switchblades. Peter's Matses friend Pepe served medicine with a large hunting knife that resembled the knife Rambo carried. Peter Gorman used an expensive chef's knife when he served sapo. It is very important that the instrument used to scrap off the dried sapo is clean and sterile.

The secretion of the giant monkey tree frog and the application of the secretion is called many different names in Amazonia. The Matses that Peter Gorman met in the mid 80s called it sapo, because of their limited understanding of Spanish. Sapo in Spanish means toad, but the Matses only had one word in Spanish for all frogs and toads, and everything associated with them. Sapo was the frog, the secretion, and the act of serving/receiving the medicine. It was all known as sapo, and a lot of people in Peru, and other parts of the world still call the secretion sapo. The Matses Peter met called the frog, dow kiet, which Peter wrote about in *Sapo in My Soul*. Indigenous people in Brazil call the secretion kambo, and kambo has become the more known name in the western world.

Morgan Maher wrote in *Sapo in My Soul*, "It is sapo, and it is kambo. It is amphibian, in our bodies, souls and worlds." I refer to the secretion as sapo, because that is the name that Peter used. Sapo, kambo, kampo, kampu are just a few of the names for the secretion from the giant monkey tree frog. It is also known as Vacina da Floresta (vaccine of the forest). There are a lot of tribes in Amazonia, and each tribe has their own nomenclature. So it's not unusual for something to be called many different names all across Amazonia.

Peter Gorman often wrote about the differences between sapo and kambo on his blog. He taught both application methods in the practitioner courses he offered. According to Peter, the main difference is that sapo is known to originate from Peru, while the kambo method is known to come from Brazil. The secretion is the same, but the applications of the secretion are different. Sapo is a method in which human saliva is used as a mixing agent to liquefy the dried secretion into a paste. In kambo, water is used as a mixing agent to liquefy the dried secretion into a paste.

Another difference is when receiving kambo the participant will usually drink water before the medicine is served, and with sapo, no water is consumed. There are practitioners today who refer to not consuming water as "dry kambo". It varies, but typically the amount of water served is one to two liters. Some of the reasoning behind the water consumption is that it allows the body to quickly release toxins from the body. Peter always said that he preferred sapo, because it would work more on your whole body, instead of just focusing on the stomach because you had a liter of water in there.

The Katukina and Yawanawa tribes in Brazil have a drink called caicuma before they experience kambo. Caicuma is a fermented drink prepared by chewing corn, yuca, or sweet potato. Several tribes in Amazonia consume fermented drinks made with banana, corn, yuca, or papaya juice before receiving the secretion. Peter Gorman told me that he never once saw a Matses just drink water. He said he only saw them drink water that was fermented with corn, yuca, or other jungle fruits, but never just plain water. The Matses that Peter Gorman met in the 80s didn't consume any water or fermented liquids before receiving sapo.

Peter wrote on 9/23/18:

Another explanation of water with sapo/ kambo. Thought I just wrote about this but then today someone asked if it was necessary to drink a gallon of water prior to sapo/kambo use. This is what I wrote: If you do the medicine Matses style, sapo style, there is no drinking of water beforehand.

But the Matses were hunters/gathers when I met them, still eating tree barks for carbohydrates because they did not have fields. They would put pineapple tops down on hunting paths and such, but they were not yet agrarian. What they needed sapo for was to clean them out, steady their hand with a bow and arrow, allow them to walk several days with little sleep, little food, and little water. Now the Brazilian groups that we subsequently learned about who used sapo, did it kambo style: The Katukina and Yaminawa were more agrarian and fishermen and less depending on hunting. So it might be - - and this is only my hypothesis - - that they suffered more stomach ailments because of their diet, and so needed the kambo to clean their stomachs out. Their style emphasized drinking water - - one or two liters, never a gallon, which could kill a person who weighed under 100 lbs - - to help produce vomiting, which would clean out the stomach of rotten material.

In the western world, human saliva is often seen as repugnant, and mixing anything with saliva is considered a social taboo. However, human saliva is not harmful. Human saliva is 99.5% water, and contains lots of beneficial substances like electrolytes, antimicrobial enzymes, and antiviral compounds. Salivary antimicrobial peptides are the first line of defense in the oral and gastrointestinal system, and instinctive wound licking occurs in both humans and animals. We have all seen cats and dogs lick their wounds, and there are many stories throughout history of people being healed by someone licking their wounds. The enzymes in human saliva quickly breaks down the peptides in sapo making them more available for the body to absorb.

In Northwest Amazonia, it is a part of life to use saliva for drinks and medicine. In the jungle they chew yuca to make masato, the sacred drink of Amazonia made from chewed and fermented yuca. Masato goes back at least a thousand years before the Incas, and long before the Spanish arrived.

Masato is made by boiling yuca (also called cassava or manioc), and then peeling, and mashing it. It is usually made by women who chew the mashed yuca, sometimes chewing a mouthful for up to thirty minutes before spitting the yuca into a bucket. The saliva enzymes help transform the starch into sugar. After it's chewed, you let it set for two or three days, and the human saliva allows the fermentation process to take place. If it is made for children, it is not fermented. Masato will give you a buzz, and that's why some call it jungle beer. It can also give you energy, allowing you to work long hours without getting hungry or tired. Masato is consumed in the jungle, and up in the Andes Mountains by workers engaged in strenuous agricultural labor. Some say that's it's magical, and that it's a secret that's been passed down by their ancestors. I've heard a few Peruvians say that most Westerners are too dumb to understand masato. I can't say that I really enjoyed the taste of masato, which reminded me of sour milk, but I am open to more research.

There's a corn beer that's made in parts of South America called chicha de jora that involves chewing corn, and spitting the corn into water so that it will ferment. The saliva allows the fermentation process to begin. The corn is left in large vats for several days, and the length of the fermentation determines the flavor. It has a yellow color and has a sour aftertaste like a grainy apple cider. It is most popular in Bolivia, Columbia, Ecuador, and Peru. Chicha de jora has a low alcohol content, 1-4% abv. Archaelogists estimate that chicha de jora dates back to around 5000 B.C. Chicha de jora was a sacred drink of the Incas, and they drank buckets of it during religious ceremonies and rites of passage. The Incas believed that sharing chicha de jora was an act of friendship and understanding. Chicha is still very popular in the Sacred Valley of Peru, and sold in small rural homes called chicherias. These chicherias have wooden tables and dirt floors, and when the chicha de jora is ready, the chicherias put out a red flag letting customers know.

"Our point? That something feels natural or unnatural doesn't mean that it is. Every one of the examples above, including saliva beer, is savored somewhere, by folks who would be disgusted by much of what you eat regularly. Especially when we're talking about intimate, personal, biological experiences like eating or having sex, we must not forget that the familiar fingers of culture reach deep into our minds. We can't feel them adjusting our dials and flicking our switches, but every culture leads its members to believe some things are naturally right and others naturally wrong. These beliefs may feel right, but it's a feeling we trust at our own peril."
    - Dr. Christopher Ryan, *Sex at Dawn*

Being prepared for a sapo session enables you to fully engage in the experience, and increases the likelihood of achieving your goals with the experience. In the days leading up to a sapo experience, it is advisable to follow a clean diet to lessen the strain on the body, potentially making the experience less challenging. It is best to avoid alcohol, dairy, sugar, and spicy foods. Do not abstain from salt in the days before a sapo session, a diet consisting of mineral-rich sea salt will make sure that you have the proper electrolytes for the experience. Sapo can disturb electrolyte balances in the body especially when you add water into the experience. Insufficient sodium in your blood can lead to hyponatremia, a condition that can be avoided with a diet of whole foods like fruit and vegetables prior to a frog medicine experience.

It is advised to refrain from consuming any food, medication, or supplements several hours before a sapo session. It is optimal to experience sapo on an empty stomach, but it is not advisable to fast for an extended period of time before the session. You want to stay hydrated, but do not drink excessive amounts of water. Participants with unstable blood sugar should consider receiving sapo in the morning, so the fasting is not as much of an issue. Peter observed that often in Matses culture sapo was often received before meals or a couple hours after them, with no special preparation, and he also told me stories about his Matses teachers doing sapo right after eating a big meal. Peter said that sometimes the Matses he observed just did it when they felt like they needed to do it.

The dosage range for most people is one to four dots of sapo. Typically, the larger the person, the larger the dose. A person weighing one-hundred pounds will not need as much sapo as someone weighing two-hundred pounds. Experience can be a factor in the dosage amount as well. I did not witness anyone receive more than five dots of sapo during my time around Peter. I've heard people brag about receiving a lot of dots, but those people were most likely receiving dots in kambo style, not sapo. The most sapo Peter Gorman witnessed anyone receive was the time his friend Juan received ten dots to stop an irregular heart beat. Right after the tenth dot was applied Juan blacked out, and rolled down a hill. He was passed out for several hours, but afterwards he was fine, and those ten dots cured his irregular heart beat. Peter Gorman told me that he received nine burns one time, and it was one of the worst experiences of his life. He said that he would never recommend going through that much pain.

When a practitioner uses saliva (sapo style), the client will require fewer dots than when using water (kambo style), as diluting the secretion with water requires more of it to produce the same effect. And typically with kambo, the burns/dots are smaller than the ones you receive with sapo, which means you will need more kambo dots than your average sapo serving. I witnessed a few people ask Peter for ten dots. He would give them three, and it would kick their ass. No way they could have handled ten burns from Peter. I have read that some members of the Katukina tribe receive one-hundred dots of kambo at a time. That sounds crazy, but remember that most of the Katukina tribal members have been using kambo since they were small children, so their bodies have built up the strength and tolerance to handle such massive dosages. I don't think it is necessary to take such heroic dosages with the frog secretion. In fact, it can be dangerous, and even fatal.

Most people who have never received sapo before worry about the burn, but the burn is the easy part. It's funny how quickly someone forgets about the burn once the sapo gets into their system. The Matses use a small twig of tamishi vine to burn the outer layer of skin. They use some type of heating source such a cigarette lighter or a torch to get the end of the tamishi red hot. Once it's hot enough, it is applied to the skin. It's doesn't have to be deep or held on the skin very long. It should just be a quick poke to break the outer layer of the skin. Breaking this layer of skin will allow the sapo to enter the bloodstream immediately, making you feel the effects within a few seconds.

After the skin has been burned, the outer layer of skin needs to be removed. It can be gently rubbed off using your finger, and it is advised to not use your fingernails. The size of the burn depends on the size of the tamishi vine that is used. Burns can range in size from the tip of a small felt pen to almost a dime. Peter Gorman preferred using large pieces of tamishi, so receiving two dots from Peter was like getting four from someone else.

The experience begins with the sapo being placed onto the skin where the outer layer has been removed. The upper arms and chest are the traditional body locations for Matses men to receive sapo. The Matses women usually receive sapo on their lower legs. I observed Peter Gorman serve it to people in different spots all over the body. A lot of women receive sapo on their lower back and legs, because they didn't want the burn marks on their arms. There's definitely more than one way to receive the medicine. Modern practitioners have started applying it to the chakras areas of the body. The chakra refers to the energy points of the body. There has been no scientific research to determine the effects of applying sapo on the chakra points. Peter Gorman said that it is best to stay away from points close to the heart. One time on the boulevard in Iquitos I watched a man receive several sapo dots on his forehead. He was fine afterwards, but I don't believe that receiving sapo on the face is a good idea.

In recent years the *New York Times* had an article that described this frog experience as "a thermonuclear-scale raw celery cleanse".

I would say that in most cases that is an over-the-top description. Your experience depends on the state of your body, mind, and spirit. It also depends on the environment where you receive the medicine, who administers the sapo, and the dosage you receive. Every sapo experience is different because the body, mind, and spirit is constantly changing. The peptides in sapo will trigger the body to work on the parts that need help.

Peter Gorman wrote in *Sapo in My Soul: The Matses Frog Medicine*:

If you've ever had a niacin flush, you've had a glimpse of what sapo will do in terms of cleansing your body from the inside out. As the medicine moves through your bloodstream, it loosens the plaque buildup in your arteries that causes diminished blood flow and can lead to heart disease. Similarly, it cleans out the fat, dirt, and dead skin in your body's pores, allowing your skin to breathe as it was meant to breathe. It rushes through your system eliminating all of the toxins that block, clog, and otherwise diminish the functions of our organs. Over the years I've seen it improve general vigor in people, permanently improve eyesight, eliminate heart palpitations, and ease the pain of rheumatoid arthritis, all by opening up the blood flow.

The session begins once the sapo is placed on the body. You will feel it burn within a minute. When Peter served sapo, he had his assistants remove the sapo from the participants arms at eleven minutes. Sessions generally last around fifteen to twenty minutes. Some experiences are longer depending on several factors such as: 1.) the condition mentally, physically, and spiritually of the participant 2.) the experience of the practitioner 3.) the source of the medicine 4.) the location it's being served 5.) the number of burns 6.) the size of the burns.

You could argue for some other factors, but these are the main ones. I've had some experiences that have lasted for hours, so it's wise to always be prepared to set aside enough time to fully recover. Even though my experience may only last fifteen to twenty minutes, I always set aside two hours. At times, it might take an hour before I can stand up and move around, and then I might need another hour before I feel prepared to engage in activities that require cognitive functioning and decision-making. Typically, after two hours, my body and mind are ready to function in the real world again.

Every session is different, but not every session is difficult. Sometimes the experience will be beautiful, and nothing but bliss. It does get easier the more you experience it. But sometimes your face and throat may swell, and you may wrinkle up like a Shar Pei, not likely but it is possible. You may sweat a lot. You may experience nausea and vomiting within a few minutes. Your heart may race. You might get dizzy, and you might need to defecate. After receiving sapo some people may experience symptoms such as: abdominal pain, difficulty in swallowing, diarrhea, nausea, vomiting, runny nose, facial flush, changes in blood pressure, rapid heart rate, loss of bladder control, muscle contractions, and sweating. Some might notice facial swelling, swollen lips and tongue, a condition I like to call "frog face". The swelling is because the body releases fluids and toxins into the facial area during the sapo experience. Usually the swelling goes down after fifteen to twenty minutes of receiving the sapo.

I have seen it last for longer periods of time in certain people, but the swelling eventually goes down. I did hear a report of a woman who received sapo shortly after a botox treatment. This woman experienced swelling in the facial area for several hours, but eventually her face returned to normal.

The side effect of sapo that most people are worried about is the vomiting. They watch videos of people violently throwing up in buckets after experiencing sapo, and it scares them. Most of the time the videos you'll find online are people vomiting up water during a kambo session. I recommend people vomit, if they need to, and to not hold it in. Peter always said that it was not necessary to vomit during a sapo session to receive the benefits. The peptides are going to do their job regardless of whether you vomit or not. If you do vomit, this is a good thing because that means your body is eliminating something that did not belong there. And after I attended a few group sapo sessions, the sound of vomit hitting the bottom of a plastic bucket became the most normal sound.

"Is it necessary to drink lots of water prior to sapo/kambo use?" The answer is: If you want to concentrate the medicine on cleansing the stomach, drinking a liter of water will ensure vomiting, and probably vomiting bile. If you want a full body detox and reset, do not drink water, and do not worry about vomiting, because the Matses never thought of that as necessary for the medicine to do the work."
- Peter Gorman

There are actually many benefits that come with vomiting, such as getting rid of toxins, and allowing the body to regenerate. The act of vomiting is also considered by some as a spiritual effect because the purging can have a powerful impact on the idea of leaving something behind in the bucket. It is also important to know that while vomiting is not mandatory, there are cases where not vomiting can be an issue. For instance, if someone has drank a lot of water before a session, it is important for their safety that they vomit, so they do not develop hyponatremia or electrolyte imbalances. In some cases it might be useful to make yourself throw up using a finger. Another reason that vomiting is good, is that a significant amount of gastric juices might be released into the gut, and it's not ideal to have those toxins released back into the bloodstream.

Following the session some practitioners offer sangre de grado to aid in wound healing, and to seal the wound from any unwanted energies. Sangre de grado or dragon's blood is a tree sap from the dragon tree in the Amazon rainforest that has been used for thousands of years to treat skin wounds. It is recommended after the experience that you should drink plenty of fluids, and eat something light like fruits to get electrolytes back into the body. Exercise is a good idea after a sapo session, as is meditation, and yoga or any activity that gets the blood flowing. Sapo can reset the body to function like the body is supposed to function. Some results are instant, while other results need time and additional treatments. It might take a few days to adjust to the new you.

One of the reasons that each session is different, is because every sapo stick is different. Most sticks have at least three different frog secretions on the stick, and there will also be "hotspots" within the dried secretion on each stick. Meaning that areas of the stick will be stronger, because each frog's secretion is different.

After the session is over you might feel many side effects such as: cramps, dehydration, disorientation, fatigue, itchy skin, muscle weakness, spasms, and short-term memory loss. It is possible that someone may not feel anything at all after receiving sapo. One time I witnessed a giant body builder type take three dots of sapo from Peter Gorman, and not feel a thing. I received two dots from the same stick, and it floored me. During the session I was on all fours vomiting off Peter's front porch.

In Peru, according to all of the reports that I've seen, the giant monkey tree frogs are in great shape. The population of frogs found in the wild remains high, and the giant monkey tree frogs, with their unique secretion, seem to exhibit a higher resistance to disease than other frogs. I am hopeful for the future of amphibians, but amphibian populations are declining faster than birds and mammals.

4
Jungle Medicine in the Western World: The Amphibian Future

One of the intense pleasures of travel and one of the delights of enthographic research is the opportunity to live amongst those who have not forgotten the old ways, who still feel their past in the wind, touch it in the stones polished by rain, taste it in the bitter leaves of plants.
- Wade Davis

A question I'm frequently asked is, "What's in that frog stuff?" This frog secretion is not some new-age snake oil, but the reality is that there has been very limited research conducted on sapo. And most of that research has been done on animals or in petri dishes, not with human beings. Constantin Tastevin's 1925 anthropological report described how the tribes known as the Kachinaua, Kanamari, and Kurina referred to the secretion as "campon".

Tastevin wrote in his report:

"The amphibians are legion. Most notable is the campon of the Kachinaua. The Kachinaua, Kurina, and Kanamari tie it up alive, limbs splayed, and hold it over a fire. It's body oozes a secretion that is collected on small sticks and saved. Then they release the poor animal, for if it were to die the goo would take revenge on its tornmentors. When a native falls ill, becomes thin, pale and swollen; when he has long been unlucky in hunting, it is because there is an evil force in the body that must be expelled. Early in the morning, before dawn, while still fasting, the sick and the unlucky make small scars on their arm or stomach with the red-hot tip of a brand and then inoculate themselves with the "milk" of the toad, as they call it. They are soon seized with nausea and diarrhea: the evil force exits the body by all the orrifices: the sick man gains weight and regains his color, the unlucky one encounters more game than he can bring back: not one animal escapes his keen eyesight, his ear perceives the slightest sounds, and his weapon does not miss single target.

I attended one of these cleansing among the Kurina, as the headwaters of the Erie, the patients took the "campon" around 5 am, some of them for amusement; at 7 am they were fully recovered, and at 8 am, one of them went out hunting and returned with just one jacou (bird). The Kachinaua get up early in the morning, around 4 am. While the women prepare the first meal, grind corn and peanuts, cook bananas and yuca and do housework, men indulge in their magical rituals to ward off bad luck. One burns bird feather and hair from wild game and bathes in the smoke, in which he also thrust his weapons, another inoculates himself with the secretion of the campon. At daybreak, everyone is ready: some go off to work, others go fishing or hunting."

In October of 1969 *National Geographic* writer, photographer, and explorer Loren McIntyre landed by float plane on the Javary River. He set up camp on a riverbank near the headwaters of the Javary. He was supposed to be picked up in three days, but after only a few hours, Loren met several members of the Matses tribe, all of them dressed traditionally with tattooed faces. The Matses at this time were still known as the Mayoruna in the western world. These Matses invited him to follow them into the jungle, so he did. After a while, Loren realized that he was lost, and he had no way of making it back to his camp. Loren spent almost a month with this tribe, and witnessed many parts of Matses life including their rituals with the giant monkey tree frog. Loren watched in amazement as the tribe collected a secretion from dozens of frogs in wooden bowls, and then drank the secretion. He reported that these Matses also licked, and sucked the secretion off the frogs. He watched them slice cuts into their arms with sharp knives, and pour the secretion into the cuts. Loren didn't experience the frog medicine. Petru Popescu interviewed Loren McIntyre for the book, *Amazon Beaming:*

The chonta palm knife is passed around. Other huacas and some of the warriors open their skin to the drug. About half prefer ingestion. When did they catch those frogs? How long did they keep them in the box, collecting their skin fluids? I was entirely unaware of the operation. How much is happening in this community at all times that I, more than just a guest now, am still not able to detect? I ask about those who took the frog potion. They will be out of commission at least until tonight. But the effect of the frog potion, while more massive, is nonrecurrent, while the inhaled stuff, according to Cambio, wakes up inside the body every few hours, offering a quick and semi-sober reliving of the initial plunge. It only wears off completely in a couple of days, which is why he prefers the hunting powder.

Sapo was first researched by scientists in the 1970s, and the first scientist to study the giant monkey tree frog was the Italian pharmacologist/scientist Vittorio Erspamer (1909- 1999). This man was a very well known name in the world of pharmacology. He was nominated for the Nobel Prize twice in his lifetime, and is most widely known for being the person credited with discovering serotonin in the body. Serotonin is a neurotransmitter that helps regulate happiness and well being, and affects moods such as anxiety, sleep, appetite, temperature, and sex. Serotonin is vital for our existence as human beings. Erspamer started studying the giant monkey tree frog in 1979, and he was doing research at the University of Rome in 1990 when he received a package in the mail from Peter Gorman. The box contained a giant monkey tree frog, and a sapo stick from the Matses, along with photos from Peter's trip to the jungles of northeastern Peru.

Erspamer studied the frog, and wrote back to Peter that it was the phyllomedusa bicolor tree frog, and the secretion from the frog was a sort of fantastic chemical cocktail with many potential medical applications. Erspamer went on to say that sapo contained several dozen peptides, and that seven of those peptides were bioactive. Bioactive means the receptors in the body reacts as if the human body created these peptides found in the secretion. It works like a lock and key, and the right key can trigger certain chemical reactions, so the body can heal itself.

Vittorio Esrpamer wrote in a letter to Peter Gorman in 1990:

"It may be reasonably concluded that the intense peripheral cardiovascular and gastrointestinal symptoms observed in the early phase of sapo intoxication may be entirely ascribed to the known bioactive peptides occurring in large amounts in the frog material."

The peptides that Erspamer wrote about were: Adenoregulin, Demorphin, Deltorphin, Phyllocaerulin, Phyllomedusin, Phyllokinin, Sauvagine. Peptides are strings of amino acids. Many different types of peptides are found in the body, and all of these peptides play different roles. Research indicates that bioactive peptides may lower blood pressure, kill microbes, reduce inflammation, prevent the formation of blood clots, improve immune function. Today people are using peptide supplements to slow down the aging process, build strength & mass, prevent age-related bone loss, and improve wound healing.

Erspamer's letter to Gorman:

"It may be reasonably concluded that the intense peripheral cardiovascular and gastrointestinal symptoms observed in the early phase of sapo intoxication may be entirely ascribed to the known bioactive peptides occurring in large amounts in the frog material."

"Increase in physical strength, enhanced resistance to hunger and thirst, and more generally, increase in the capacity to face stress situations- may be explained by the presence of phyllocaeruelin and sauvagine in the drug."

"phyllomedusin and phyllokinin may increase the permeability of the blood-brain barrier, thus facilitating access to the brain not only of themselves but also of the other active peptides."

Hopefully we are headed towards a future with research on these peptides. Phyllomedusin affects these parts of the body: bowels, intestines, salivary glands, and tear ducts. Phyllomedusin contracts muscles, and causes the purging during a sapo experience. Adenoregulin is known to kill fungi, and contains a bunch of microorganisms. Phyllocaeruelin stimulates the adrenal cortex, and the pituitary glands, and acts as a digestive aid that increases secretions in the stomach, gall bladder, and pancreas. Sauvagine also stimulates the adrenal cortex, and has a long lasting effect of lowering blood pressure.

Erspamer found medical uses for dermophin and deltorphin. Both of these peptides are very potent opioid peptides that are almost identical to the endophorins that your body creates when you experience pain. Dermophin and deltorphin are similar to morphine, but without the withdrawal or addictive risks, and much stronger.

Deltorphin is also know to have a high blood-brain barrier penetration rate, and is also being researched for its ability to inhibit the growth of cancer and tumors. Dermorphin was first isolated from the skin of the giant monkey tree frog by Erspamer in 1981. Dermorphin is not found in humans or any other mammals on earth. It has only been found in amphibians, bacteria, and mollucs. In the early 80s many pharmacological papers were published on dermorphin, and in 1985 a groundbreaking study on post-operative pain management was released. It showed dermorphin's superiority over morphine. Patients in the study needed less dermorphin than they did morphine to manage pain, and dermorphin lasted longer than morphine. Dermorphin was found to have less tolerance than morphine, caused fewer withdrawal symptoms, and didn't induce sleep like morphine does. No follow up studies were ever done after this study. Interest in dermorphin had peaked in 1985, and interest has declined ever since. Dermorphine has recently been in the news for being used illegally in horse racing to make horses run faster.

Sapo is considered a non-addictive substance because the peptides are bioactive, which means that the receptor sites in the body simply shut down instead of requiring more, as in the case with opiate use. Erspamer didn't believe that sapo was a psychedelic. Erspamer wrote, "no hallucinations, visions, or 'magic' effects are produced by the known peptide components of sapo." Erspamer went on to write about how the peptides could be used as anti-inflammatories, blood pressure regulators, digestive aids, and for stimulating the adrenal cortex and the pituitary gland. The possibilities are endless for this medicine. Corporations are working hard behind the scenes on the peptides found in sapo. They have several patents on these peptides today, and developing more every day looking for the next Viagra that they can mass market to the American public. This development has contributed to controversies surrounding biopiracy and the uncompensated exploitation of indigenous knowledge.

The First Recorded Experience with sapo in 1986 on the Rio Galvez in Peru:

And it wasn't just my hearing that had been improved. My vision, my sense of smell, everything about me felt larger than life, and my body felt immensely strong. When I saw Pablo later I explained what I was feeling with hand gestures as much as language. He smiled.

"Bi-ram-bo sapo." he said, " fuerte."

It was good sapo. Strong. During the next few days, the feeling of strength didn't diminish. Both Steve and I could go whole days without being hungry or thirsty and move through the jungle for hours without tiring. Every sense I possessed was heightened and in tune with the environment, as though the sapo put the rhythm of the jungle into my blood. I could see animals before they saw me and sense which plants were benevolent and which were not, particularly the chawki paujil - named after the bird - a vine that produces drinkable water but looks very similar to other vines that can poison you.
- Peter Gorman, *Sapo in My Soul*

Frogs have been used in traditional medicine all through recorded history. They have been used in remedies for allergies, bites, cancer, heart issues, hemorrhages, HIV, infections, inflammation, and pain. Over the past sixty years frogs have played important roles in several Nobel- prizewinning experiments. John Gurdon cloned a frog in 1962, and frogs have played a crucial role in stem cell research ever since. Researchers have been using the skin of the golden poison dart frog of Columbia to better understand how to treat the human nervous system. The golden poison dart frog is tiny, about an inch long, but is considered one of the most toxic animals on Earth, and contains enough poison in their skin to kill ten adults. Researchers have been studying the poison to better understand the role electrical impulses play in processes like heart function and the sensation of pain. There has been a synthetic version of one of the poison's compounds developed that has potential as a powerful painkiller. There are more than one-hundred dart frog species, and most of them have not been studied. In 1974 John W. Daley discovered the alkaloid epibatidine in a poison dart frog from Ecuador, and in studies with mice, epibatidine was shown to be two-hundred times more potent than morphine at blocking pain in mice. Unfortunately, epibatidine also caused seizures and even death in mice, and has been proven to be too toxic for human use.

In 1987 it was discovered that the African clawed frog contained natural antibiotic compounds that were active against many disease causing organisms, and these compounds may help provide cures to future antibiotic-resistant bacteria. Scientists discovered in the 1930s that the African clawed frog could be used to test for pregnancy in women. There have been experiments done in Australia that has demonstrated that certain natural compounds found in frog secretions repealed mosquitos. The southern gastric brooding frog was studied because it produced a hormone that allowed the frog to halt digestion, and the production of stomach acids while it raised its young in its stomach. The southern gastric brooding frog gave birth out of its mouth, and was the only known species to reproduce in this way. Medical researchers wanted to study this hormone in research on treating stomach ulcers, but the frog has not been seen in the wild in over forty years. Frogs are an essential part of our existence, and they will continue to make more contributions to science as more studies are done on the thousands of compounds found in frog secretions.

After Vittorio Erspamer's research very little follow up has been done, and this research is needed to better understand how sapo can interact with different health conditions in humans. While the anecdotal evidence of sapo is exciting, more scientific research is needed for it to become a part of modern healthcare programs. Some of the short term effects of sapo can include change in mood, increased energy, greater awareness, improved mental clarity, and relief from anxiety and depression. Long term effects can include the boosting of the immune system, improved concentration, increased stamina, and upgraded circulation.

Sapo has been documented to eliminate fungi from the body, aid in the treatment of migraines, and rid the body of candida. The peptides in sapo stimulate the body to produce more endorphins, leading to an increase in serotonin production, which can help alleviate pain. Two of the peptides in sapo, cuerulein and sauvagine, are known to cause long term drop in blood pressure. There are also individuals who have reported reversing multiple sclerosis with the help of frog medicine. I spoke with several sapo practitioners who had worked with people suffering from drug addictions like alcohol, anti-depressants, cocaine, and heroin. Peter told me stories about how people he knew had brought their children over to his house for a week or two to get them off heroin addictions.

Some individuals after sapo sessions have reported receiving: calmness, clarity of mind, clearing of trauma, compassion, courage, energy, euphoria, focus, grounding, healing of sickness, heightened awareness, increased stamina, personal sovereignty, reduced stress, recharge, reconnection, reset, and stability.

I have been documenting frog medicine in the United States over the last ten years and I have heard sapo reported as a method to manage many different ailments and disorders. It is important to remember that each person is different, and every body reacts different to frog medicine. This book features many personal accounts of frog medicine experiences. Readers should know that these stories are anecdotal and not clinical proof of the medicine's effectiveness for Western ailments.

Many users believe that sapo treatments can assist the body in releasing negative energy by allowing the expulsion of low vibrational energy, and inviting more positivity into one's life. Sapo may help to clear energy blocks in your body, providing an opportunity for your body, mind, and spirit to reset and rebalance. Sapo is regarded as a potent antibiotic that is highly effective against parasites, aiding in their removal from the body. Multiple individuals have told me that they have eliminated parasites from their body after undergoing sapo treatments. Sapo can assist in clearing blockages in arteries and veins, leading to improved oxygen flow to the brain. The enhanced oxygen flow to the brain typically results in improved memory for most individuals. Sapo can also increase the blood circulation in the body by dilating blood vessels.

The Indigenous tribes that use sapo have reported they use it to overcome panema. Panema is often described as a dark energy cloud that surrounds the aura of a person. Panema can be the result of ancestral patterns, or heavy emotions caused by trauma that a person experiences in life. Panema can manifest as anxious behavior, bad luck, depression, feeling lost, irritation, lack of clarity, laziness, and other adverse states. Some groups believe that panema is a spiritual disease caused by negative energy in the body, and when panema is cleared from the body, the negative energies are removed. Removing panema can help life flow more naturally by allowing a person to move forward in life, and making it easier to overcome obstacles.

The Matses will use sapo when they are not experiencing good luck in their hunting, and the animal spirits are not communicating with them. They believe the magic of hunting will align after they have experienced the medicine. In the western world the medicine helps people find a way to increase compassion and courage while providing an outlet to release anger, fear, frustration, and self-doubt. Some believe that it realigns our chakras, and changes attitudes and patterns of health. We all go through periods where we are in a more negative state. And by negative, I mean feelings of anger, anxiety, fear, jealousy, sadness, stress, and worry. These feelings can put you in a negative state that attracts bad things into our life. Sapo can help release these negative feelings. Sapo can provide more clarity to a person's thinking, and understanding of the world while providing a grounding feeling that allows a person to be less in the head and more in their body. I have always thought of a sapo session as a tuneup for my body. Sapo gives people a chance to awaken the body's potential, and the peptides help restore the natural functioning of the body.

Sapo has been reported to be beneficial for neuropathy. Neuropathy is a disorder that is caused by nerve damage, and causes pain, numbness, and weakness. I witnessed sapo help neuropathy in my friend Mollie, who was a seventy year-old Irish lady with stage 4 cancer. She had developed neuropathy in her feet and legs from the chemotherapy she was receiving for stage 4 cancer. Neuropathy causes problems for the nervous system by making it difficult to send messages from the brain to the feet and legs. Before the neuropathy, Mollie used to walk three miles a day in a park along the Trinity River near her home in Fort Worth. Her neuropathy had gotten so bad that she could barely get out of bed. One of her friends had suggested that she try sapo, and after a few treatments, she was back to walking along the Trinity. She would always wait thirty days after chemotherapy before starting her sapo sessions.

Another health condition that sapo has been credited with helping is gout. Gout is a form of arthritis that occurs when there is a buildup of uric acid in the joints. Some practitioners use localized treatments on the fingers and toes to help balance the systems of those suffering with gout, and they believe that sapo helps get rid of the buildup of uric acid in the joints. I am aware of a case where a thirty-seven year-old man received frog medicine, which helped him overcome seventeen years of suffering with excruciating pain and discomfort caused by gout. His condition had deteriorated to the point where walking had become a challenging task for him. After undergoing treatments with frog medicine, he felt rejuvenated and revitalized, as if he were a young man again.

Lyme disease is a big problem in the United States, and there has been lots of time and money spent to study this disease. Caitlin Thompson, a neurobiologist and researcher at the UC San Diego School of Medicine, used kambo to heal from a chronic health condition that included Lyme disease, chronic fatigue syndrome, bacterial infections, depression, pain, and food sensitivity issues. Many practitioners believe that the anti-inflammatory and antimicrobial peptides in sapo are the perfect weapon to fight against Lyme disease.

"I would personally say from my own experience with Lyme and Lyme clients, that kambo is one of the most powerful interventions available today for those suffering from Lyme disease. While true clinical research with kambo is nonexistent, there are thousands of anecdotal reports of those afflicted with Lyme disease having substantial improvement after the use of kambo." - Caitlin Thompson

There are lots of stories out there about individuals healing different health conditions, but all of these conditions are a case by case basis, and what works for some people, may not work for others. It is important to remember: **THIS MEDICINE IS NOT FOR EVERYONE**.

There are several risk factors involved with sapo/kambo treatments. The treatments can be an intense physical experience, and might not be suitable for those in a weakened state. There are also are also several contraindications that come with sapo. Contraindication is to withhold certain medical treatment due to the harm it could cause the patient. The effects of sapo can induce panic and distress, but an experienced practitioner should be able to handle any distress. Sapo is a potent vasodilator, and can cause changes in blood pressure and heart rate. Every situation and person is different, but it is advised for people who suffer from the following health conditions to avoid sapo for risk of serious side effects:

Serious heart issues
History of blood clots, strokes or aneurysm
Recovering from major surgery
Taking medication for low blood pressure
Person lacking the mental capacity to make the decision to take it.
History of serious mental illness such as schizophrenia
Pregnant or breast feeding a child
Under 18 years of age
Have Addison's disease
Have epilepsy
Taking immune-suppressants after organ transplant
Have done chemotherapy or radiotherapy in the past month

Because of the limited amount of research, and case studies done with sapo, it is best to be cautious when considering the use of this ordeal medicine. It is a very challenging and powerful medicine. It can facilitate deep growth and healing, but that comes at a price. There are dangers associated with experiencing any "ordeal" medicine, but adverse or allergic reactions are rare with sapo. Many practitioners recommend a test dot/point on your first experience before receiving a full dose to make sure there are not any adverse effects or allergic reactions with the medicine.

It is very important for individuals receiving sapo to discuss any medical conditions or medications they may be taking with their practitioner before undergoing the sapo experience. No session with this frog medicine is 100% safe for everybody, but statistically it is safer than driving down the freeway in Dallas, Texas. The most dangerous aspect of sapo is the risk of fainting, and causing harm to oneself. Most of the time this happens when the participant stands up to walk to the bathroom. The fainting is caused by a drop in blood pressure. I witnessed someone faint in Iquitos after being served sapo by Gorman. Luckily someone was there to catch them. This person had experienced sapo several times before, and had never fainted after sapo.

A Google search will reveal that sapo/kambo has been associated with a few deaths, with the total number being less than ten in the past twenty years. Almost all reported cases of death related to sapo/kambo have been attributed to practitioner errors or individuals undergoing the experience without a guide or sitter. Some of the deaths involved hyponatremia, caused by an excessive intake of water before, during, or after a session with the frog medicine. There were a couple of reports that involved cardiac arrest and seizures. In 2021, a man died after experiencing excessive vomiting from kambo following an ayahuasca experience. The man didn't receive medical attention in time, and died. Some of the cases involved individuals who received frog medicine after taking multiple prescription and over-the-counter drugs, as well as psychedelics. The majority of these cases could have been prevented with the implementation of proper safety measures and screening protocols.

The amphibian medicine market has exploded in the last ten years, and a lot has changed in the frog medicine world since Peter Gorman wrote about being the first westerner to put an animal product directly into the human bloodstream for medicinal purposes. Peter frequently expressed concerns about these changes during my time with him. There are many issues concerning sapo as it continues to become a bigger part of modern medicine in the western world.

And unfortunately this frog medicine has attracted a lot of charlatans looking to capitalize on an unregulated market. This rapid growth has opened the door for overnight facilitators who are not providing safe environments for their clients, and leading to concerns about the authenticity and quality of the treatments being offered. Practitioner courses are being taught over the internet, and people are not receiving enough real world experience before they start serving clients.

Peter often worried about the dangers of not teaching proper safety methods in the modern world. I recall Peter becoming quite upset when his friend Alan Shoemaker began offering practitioner courses in Iquitos in 2017. I captured some of Peter's reaction, and Peter swore that Alan hadn't experienced sapo since the early 90s in Peter's apartment in New York City. Peter was in disbelief that Allen was going to offer courses with his lack of experience working with frog medicine. He was really irritated because he had invested a lot of time in teaching westerners about sapo, and Peter had only began teaching courses the previous year. Peter and Allen were always fighting about something, and eventually they reconciled, and became best friends again.

Today there is a multitude of individuals teaching frog medicine practitioner courses all over the world. Sapo and kambo has healed many people who now seek to provide opportunities for others to heal like they did. There have been lots of criticism about the abundance of schools, and the number of sapo/kambo practitioners that are out there today. It is my opinion that it's beneficial to have established organizations where individuals can learn about safety practices, and receive practical instruction before embarking on their journey to serve frog medicine.

In 2015 Jason Fellows was searching for ayahuasca, and made the decision to travel to South America in pursuit of healing. Jason had served in the Coast Guard for six years on the border of Texas and Mexico, where most of his work involved dealing with the cartel. This line of work had taken a toll on him, and left him with a lot of fear, worries, and symptoms reminiscent of PTSD. After traveling to Peru, he came across the giant monkey tree frog, and this encounter changed his life. After experiencing frog medicine, he realized his desire to share it with others. Jason developed a relationship with the Cocama tribe in Peru, and today oversees a practitioner school called Tribal Detox that is based in Colorado. He and his partner have developed classes that train people on serving frog medicine. His school focuses on the kambo style of serving, and helping individuals safely administer kambo.

Jason grew up in Graham, Texas, the town where I was born. We didn't know each other growing up, but we did know some of the same people. It is a remarkable coincidence that two guys with connections to Graham ended up in Peru at around the same time to encounter life changing experiences with jungle medicines.

Jason would eventually introduce his cousin Tommi Dawn Chapman to kambo. Tommi Dawn was in her mid thirties when she experienced kambo for the first time. She had been suffering with a bad case of asthma her entire life, and doctors had her on multiple medications to treat it. She couldn't leave the house without an inhaler, but after one session with kambo she didn't need it anymore. Following a few more sessions, she was completely free from her asthma, and she stopped taking her medications for it. Tommi Dawn couldn't stop sharing her story, and one Sunday morning she stood up in the First Baptist Church of Graham, and told the whole congregation, and everyone on Facebook Live that she was healed by kambo.

Emily Johnson, a lifelong resident of Graham, heard about Tommi Dawn's miraculous recovery, and was searching for relief from a chronic kidney infection that had caused her major depression. Emily decided to try kambo, and the effects were almost immediate. Emily felt like she had received a major release from depression after her first session, and she knew right then that she wanted to become a practitioner. Emily's husband Michael witnessed such a dramatic change in Emily, that one month after Emily finished her kambo practitioner course with Tribal Detox, Michael went to Colorado to take the course. Michael had suffered with back issues, carpal tunnel, and inflammation his entire adult life, and after working with kambo for several months, all of those issues began to disappear.

One of the reasons Jason started Tribal Detox was to teach safety standards, and to bring awareness to safety issues in the world of frog medicine. Peter Gorman was confident that with appropriate screening and stringent safety protocols, there should be minimal complications when receiving this medicine. As the number of practitioners grows, so does the number of individuals out there pushing the boundaries with this medicine. There are practitioners serving excessive dots, and having clients drink excessive amounts of water before, during, and after receiving kambo. This trend of excess has developed as practitioners aim to demonstrate to their clients that they have received some healing from the experience. The payoff being the vomit in the bucket, as it serves as a visible validation of the client's investment in the session. I can appreciate this viewpoint, because kambo sessions can be costly, and rightfully so. If you are working with one of the top facilitators, their expertise and energy should come at a premium price.

Today you will find frog medicine practitioners who claim that they can interpret their client's vomit, suggesting they can discern the effects of the medicine or the body's reaction based on the color of the vomit. There is no scientific evidence or studies to support the validity of interpreting the color of vomit as a reliable indicator of the body's reaction. Many believe that these claims are due to practitioners developing new marketing techniques as competition increases.

The concept of paying for a medicine that causes discomfort is a foreign notion to a lot of Americans. The majority of Americans rely on medications to prevent vomiting, and many people in the Western world have a strong fear of vomiting. Certain individuals may perceive the act of purging as a sign of vulnerability or weakness. Where I grew up we were taught to hold it in, and it will go away. Well, that suppressive backwoods bullshit didn't work for me. I saw another path. I found enlightenment when I let go, and purged it out. And I am also of the opinion that the therapeutic benefits of sapo can be achieved without the need for vomiting during a session. From my observations, individuals may experience more vomiting during their initial sapo sessions compared to after they have experienced the medicine a few times. Once again, the dosage and dietary choices leading up to the session play a significant role in determining the extent of purging that an individual may experience. If you have a preexisting condition, you may also be more prone to experiencing vomiting during a session.

Peter Gorman often expressed his opinion that the ayahuasca dieta was simply a creation of Western influence. The ayahuasca dieta is a diet that is followed before and after an ayahuasca ceremony. Peter noted that many individuals were engaging in sapo and kambo sessions following the ayahuasca dieta, and this was leading to safety concerns. Furthermore, due to the restrictions of the dieta, individuals were avoiding salt and consuming excessive amounts of water, potentially leading to electrolyte imbalances and hyponatremia. This risk can be effectively prevented by ensuring a healthy salt intake prior to a session. The ayahuasca dieta started as a joke at a restaurant in Iquitos, and eventually it caught on because of the gringos, and now everyone is offering the ayahuasca dieta. Tourists have been known to show up to retreat centers prepared for frog medicine sessions after following the ayahuasca dieta for thirty days, a decision often influenced by information they have read online.

Peter Gorman wrote in 2013:

I think that both the indigenous and non-indigenous in the Peruvian Amazon have traditionally lived primarily on a diet of fish and platanos - - with some exceptions, like the Matses and other groups who primarily ate meat, rather than fish.

So I think if a Westerner found a curandero and had not brought his/her own food supply, that they'd soon just find themselves eating fish and platano most meals. I just think that's one of the basic jungle diets. I think - - and it's only me thinking here - - that food restrictions come when new foods are introduced: if a person lived in an area where there were no hot peppers, for instance, but then went to a town where there was a jar of hot peppers in lime or sidra on the table, and then ate a spoonful, well, the shock of the heat and the burning of the mouth might make that person immediately swear off peppers and have them telling their friends and family not to eat them either. With something like pork, well, if it's not prepared well you can get awfully sick from it - - and with no refrigeration it's easy to get sick on pig in the jungle. So I think that's another pretty naturally proscribed in traditional settings where ayahuasca was served.

I think the answer to your question though, really lies more in the boom of ayahuasca drinking that's gone on over the last 10-12 years in Peru. When Francisco Montes opened Sachamama in about 1993 - - the first real ayahuasca center, I believe - - he never talked - - to me, at least, - - about dieta. Out at his place we'd eat fruit and fish; when he came to Iquitos he'd eat ceviche with me or have a soda with lots of sugar. But by 2003 or 2004, he'd build several tambos on his place specifically for dietaros - - people on the ayahuasca diet - - and was serving a pretty strict routine of boiled fish and platanos or rice.

Some of those people who spent time with Francisco went on to open their own retreats, and they used the dieta as well. Then someone like Gerald at the Yellow Rose, for a joke, put up a sign that said he served the Ayahausca Diet: No salt, no oil, no sugar, no SEX! Well, at first it was a joke, but when people started ordering it, he started to make it, which made other restaurants follow suit - - so that now all of the restaurants that serve gringos provide the ayahuasca diet. (As a side and snide comment I will add that I've talked with some of the retreat owners who relish the fact that by serving just cucumbers, fruit and some boiled fish and plantains they save a boatload of money.) So I think the dieta just sort of caught on, and that it's become a badge of courage for a lot of people."

Legality:

In 2021 Australia made kambo illegal. Kambo is listed as a schedule 10 poison, the highest possible classification for medicines and chemicals. It was made illegal after two deaths in northern New South Wales, Australia. Neither one of these cases have shown that kambo was the cause of death.

The Katukina tribe in Brazil in 2004 lobbied the Brazilian government to outlaw the advertising and sale of kambo due to intellectual property rights claimed by the Katukina tribe of Brazil. The Brazilian government was concerned with biopiracy, the theft of biological resources from country's native habitats for commercial use. People in Brazil have not forgotten how the pharmaceutical giant Bristol-Myers Squibb used the snake venom of the jararaca viper to make a blood pressure medicine called captopril, not one penny went to the indigenous people of the territory where the snake was found. The Brazilian Ministry of Health ruled than any profits from kambo must benefit Brazil. Kambo is banned for use in Brazil, except for the Katukina, and a few other indigenous tribes living in Amazonia. The secretion is legal everywhere in the world except Australia and Brazil.

Unfortunately, there is more people in need of sapo than there is sapo available. The increased popularity of the frog secretion will lead to the demand surpassing the available supply in the not too distant future. There are stories out there about frog farms where giant monkey tree frogs are over- harvested and not treated very well. This is one of the reasons why it is important to know the source of your frog medicine, and that it has been ethically harvested. Efforts are underway to develop a synthetic alternative to sapo, but the feasibility of creating a substitute remains uncertain at this time. The development of a synthetic alternative to sapo could help ease the strain on the giant monkey tree frog population while expanding access to the frog medicine.

It has been reported that the use of sapo outside the Matses culture has led to internal conflicts within the Matses tribe. It is from the Matses perspective that part of their culture is being taken away without any recognition coming back to the people that first introduced sapo to the modern world.

Additional research on the combination of substances with sapo is essential, and should be prioritized for a better understanding of potential interactions and effects. These days, most plant medicine retreat centers and practitioners offer a variety of medicines alongside sapo. If you are going to experience sapo and ayahuasca on the same day, it's best to experience sapo before an ayahuasca ceremony, and at least four to five hours before the ceremony. The optimal approach is to experience sapo in the morning, and then ayahuasca in the evening. Sapo can assist in eliminating toxins and negativity, enabling you to be more focused and receptive to information during your ayahuasca ceremony, but receiving sapo the morning after an ayahuasca ceremony can pose risks. Especially, if you have been up all night purging, as it may lead to increased physical and mental strain on the body.

Peter frequently warned about the high number of contaminated sticks being circulated for sale on the internet, urging individuals to exercise caution when searching for sources to purchase sapo sticks. They have been reports of fraudulent substances such as egg yoke and yuca juice being falsely sold as sapo. These contaminated sticks have caused people to suffer through horrible autoimmune responses. This is why it is important to always know the source of your medicine. It's good to ask questions about the sourcing of your sticks, and who collected the secretion.

Part II
The Teachings

5
MEETING THE FROG TEACHER

Look at every path closely and deliberately. Try it as many times as you think necessary. Then ask yourself, and yourself alone one question. This question is one that only a very old man asks. My benefactor told me about it once when I was young, and my blood was too vigorous for me to understand it. Now I do understand it. I will tell you what it is: Does this path have a heart? All paths are the same: they lead nowhere. They are paths going through the bush, or into the bush. In my own life I could say that I have traversed long, long paths, but I am not anywhere. My benefactor's question has meaning now. Does this path have heart? If it does, the path is good; if it doesn't, it is of no use. Both paths lead nowhere; but one has a heart, the other doesn't. One makes a joyful journey; as long as you follow it, you are one with it. The other will make you curse your life. One makes you strong; the other weakens you.
- Carlos Castaneda, *The Teachings of Don Juan: A Yaqui Way of Knowledge*

March 7, 2015 - Jack County, Texas

I ended up back at my childhood home because I decided to leave Dallas three years ago at the peak of my alcoholism. This homestead was located in the Upper Brazos River Valley: thirty miles north of the Brazos River, seventy miles south of the Red River, and a two hour drive west of Dallas. I grew up in the rock hills of western Jack County on land that was once known as Comancheria. Comanche Chiefs like Peta Nocona, and his son Quanah Parker roamed this land freely before the white settlers came to stake their claim in the mid 1850s.

Living near bars was not good for me, and Dallas had as many bars as any place in the world. After spending a decade in Dallas, I came to the realization that the city was far from an ideal setting to get sober. I was drunk most of the time from the age of eighteen until I turned thirty-five. Most nights I would black out, and the next morning I would not have a clue how I got home. There were several run-ins with the law, and countless nights I'm glad I don't remember. I needed to be in a place where time seemed to stand still, a spot where I could reflect on the past, and contemplate the future. It was a setting that felt both familiar and comforting.

When I left Dallas I had hair down past my shoulders, a huge black beard, and a pocket full of conspiracy theories that I would yap about nonstop. I didn't have a plan when I moved back home, but I knew that if I didn't alter my ways, my life was going to be a lot shorter than I wanted it to be. I began reading books about Timothy Leary, Ram Dass, Ken Kesey and the Merry Pranksters, and the psychedelic movement of the 60s. It was around this same time that my friend Dax Norman told me about this podcast with the stand-up comic Joe Rogan. I knew him as the *Fear Factor* and *NewsRadio* guy. The first podcast I listened to had Graham Hancock discussing his experiences drinking ayahuasca in Brazil with an indigenous tribe.

This was the first time that I had heard the word ayahuasca since an anthropology course I had taken in college at Southwest Texas State University (now Texas State). The course was called Magic, Ritual, and Religion, and it was a hard class to get into, because everybody wanted to take a class about magic and drugs. It was taught by Dr. Jim Garber, who reminded me of a modern day Indiana Jones. He was a very charismatic professor who told us lots of stories about traveling to archaeological sites in Central and South America. These stories were riveting to a twenty-two year old who had never been outside the United States. The class covered indigenous cultures, and their use of plant medicines. Magic, Ritual, and Religion was the only class that I would not skip to go drink beer on the Guadalupe River. After hearing Graham Hancock talking about his ceremonies, I knew I had to get to South American. I immediately started reading and listening to everything I could find about ayahuasca.

One positive result from my alcoholism was that I became delusional enough to pursue a childhood dream of becoming a filmmaker. I started networking and volunteering at film festivals, and working on low budget independent films shot around Dallas/Ft. Worth. I worked on documentaries, live concerts, music videos, westerns, and short films. I watched every Werner Herzog and Errol Morris film that I could find. I had been studying filmmaking and writing scripts for the last twelve years. I first learned about Peter Gorman shortly after my thirty-sixth birthday in 2013, when a friend stopped by and left me a copy of his book, *Ayahuasca in My Blood: 25 Years of Medicine Dreaming.* I opened the book after my friend left, and began skimming through it when I read, "Lives in Joshua, Texas", and I just about had a heart attack. I couldn't believe that this guy lived seventy-seven miles from me in North Texas. What are the odds that a guy like Gorman lived in

Johnson County? I had a few friends from there, but all I really knew about Johnson County was that it was not a place that you would expect to find a New York Democrat.

Tomorrow I was going to Joshua to meet Peter Gorman. I would be lying if I said I wasn't nervous. It had been two years since I read his book, and I finally got the courage to talk to him. I reached out to my friend Tom Huckabee, and asked him to introduce us over email. Tom facilitated the introduction, and Peter wrote back, and invited me to come down to Joshua for a Sunday visit.

March 8, 2015 - Joshua, Texas

I had been preparing for this day for a long time. I was still astonished that someone like Gorman resided in Joshua, situated in the heart of Johnson County, a place known as one of the reddest counties in Texas. Johnson County used to lean Democratic, but these days it's ninety percent Republican, and these folks don't care too much for liberal New York writers associated with pro-drug publications like *High Times*. I was a huge fan of *High Times*, and meeting someone who actually wrote stories for that magazine was a dream come true. When you grew up before the internet during an era of cannabis prohibition,

High Times was the only mainstream news outlet advocating for cannabis, and covering topics like psychedelics.

I had been promising my Mom for a while that I was going to drive her to Alvarado to visit her sister Louise. Alvarado was just a twenty minute drive southeast of Joshua. So the next day, my Mom and I left early in the morning, and enjoyed a pleasant two hour drive to Alvarado. I dropped Mom off at Aunt Louise's, and turned north up I-35 for a few miles before exiting onto a farm-to-market road leading west towards Joshua. As I drove along the winding farm-to-market road, I was suddenly overcome by a strange feeling. I wasn't sure what was happening. I felt like I was experiencing some sort of anxiety attack, and it was coming on fast. My head was spinning, and I was shaking all over. I felt like I was going to pass out. I pulled the car over to the side of the road, and got out, and collected my thoughts. The fresh air helped ground me. After a few minutes, I was feeling better. I got back into the car, and resumed my trip to Gorman's.

Gorman lived on the outskirts of Joshua near the tollroad between Ft. Worth and Cleburne. It was a bright, sunny Sunday afternoon. I drove past the Gorman's house, made a u-turn, and parked in front of his house. There were several cars parked in his driveway behind Peter's Ford Ranger.

When Peter purchased this one acre property, he couldn't believe that he got the whole acre, along with the house, a garage, and a tiny shed where he could write novels. You didn't get that kind of space in New York City. Peter's acre lot was filled with shade from a variety of trees including oak, elm, hackberry, and cedar. At the back of his property, nestled among the shade trees, was Peter's chicken coop. Adding to the charm of his property, a gentle creek flowed with a couple of bridges that allowed him access to the west side of his lot.

The birds filled the air with their songs as I got out of my car. I was nervous as I walked up to the house. Although the anxiety had passed, I still had butterflies in my stomach. I was eager to finally meet the jungle man. As I stepped up to the front porch, I was greeted by Boots, the Gorman's dog. I don't normally pet dogs I don't know, but Boots seemed harmless, so I gave him a pat on the head, and knocked on the door.

"Come on in," Gorman yelled.

I walked into Gorman's living room, my eyes wide with excitement, and anticipation. Peter was seated at his desk, and I extended my hand for a handshake as I entered the room. Peter introduced me to the group, and I managed to offer a polite smile and wave in response. Peter's home resembled what I envisioned a jungle explorer's home to be like. There were poison blow darts hanging on the wall along with knives, and five-foot long spears. Peter had been traveling to Peru, and collecting for museums since 1984, and he had acquired a lot of Amazonian artifacts over the years.

There was an old television with dozens of trophies sitting on it that Peter had won while working as a writer for the *Fort Worth Weekly*. Two of the trophies read, "Texas Print Journalist of the Year". In the corner of the living room was a basket full of big green leaves. I found out later that they were called chakapas. A chakapa is a rattle or shaker that is constructed of leaves from the chakapa bush, and it is used by South American shamans during healing ceremonies. Curanderos and shamans use chakapas to clean the energy of the space around them.

My attention was drawn to a photograph of a man with his penis tied up against his stomach by a string that was running around his body. The man was holding a bow and arrow, and surrounded by topless women holding their babies. "That's Pablo with all his children and wives standing behind him. Pablo was one of my teachers. He had four wives, and twenty-eight children. That's Moises my guide," said Peter as he pointed at the picture, "They were still pretty wild back then, because the Matses had only been in contact with the western world since '69. They weren't wearing sneakers and Nike t-shirts yet. They still cut their hair with piranha teeth, and trapped majas. Are you hungry? There's hummus, and chips, and some fruit on the kitchen table."

The people in the room were old friends of Peter's. One was a Fort Worth born filmmaker who lived in L.A. named Paul, who had just been down to Peru on one of Peter's trips. He told me some stories about how great the trip was, and how strong the ayahuasca was down in the jungle. The other guests included a magazine editor named Mike and his wife Diane. Mike had collaborated with Peter on several stories over the years. The couple had spent a lot of Sunday afternoons in Joshua where there was always an abundance of delicious food, and lively conversation.

I was slightly disappointed to discover that Peter didn't really smoke weed. Peter mentioned that occasionally he would indulge in smoking cannabis, but even during his tenure at *High Times*, where he received an abundance of free weed, he said he didn't smoke much of it. Wine was Peter's preferred beverage, and he savored several glasses of red wine that day. Peter told me that he had given up drinking whiskey twenty-five years ago, and that he stopped drinking scotch in the eighties. Peter then confessed that a couple of times a year, he would purchase a few of those miniature airplane bottles of bourbon. He also mentioned that on rare occasions someone would buy him a bottle of high quality bourbon, and he hated to see it go to waste. Peter seemed to be very candid about his struggles with alcohol, and I could sense that he was becoming increasingly annoyed at the barrage of questions this recovering alcoholic was asking.

Peter came across as a down-to-earth guy, embodying the essence of a blue collar New Yorker who hailed from a working class Irish Catholic family. Gorman seemed genuine and authentic, with a rough around the edges demeanor that reflected his true identity as a seasoned jungle explorer. Peter was living a very quiet family life in Joshua as a single dad, while working as an investigative journalist for the *Fort Worth Weekly*. He was really devoted to his job as a journalist, and prioritized putting in the necessary time and effort that was needed to get the facts right, and the story presented with integrity and accuracy. Peter's daughter Madeleina had just entered high school, and occasionally she would take photos for Peter's stories. His ex-wife Chepa lived down the road with her two daughters, and Peter's two step-sons, Italo and Marko, lived nearby too. Peter said that his family was a support system that helped him navigate the complexities of living a double life with one foot in Texas, and the other in Peru. His extended family helped him balance these two worlds.

After hearing Peter that day I felt like his stories had to be true because nobody could make up stories like the ones he told. I could see that Peter took great pleasure in recounting these stories, and sharing his adventures with others. I recall leaving that day with the thought that it was surprising that there hadn't already been a film made about this man. I wasn't sure how to make a documentary, but I had the perfect subject for one. The universe had led me to Peter Gorman, and now I had to find a way to make this documentary.

August 23, 2015 - Joshua, Texas

This was the day that I was first introduced to the frog medicine called sapo. The day before I had received a call from my friend George Wada, a filmmaker from Arlington, who asked if I was interested in operating a camera for an interview he was conducting with our mutual friend Tom Huckabee. Tom was an award winning filmmaker who had lived and worked in Hollywood for many years. Tom had directed several of his own films, and produced films as the head of Bill Paxton's production company in Los Angeles. The interview was with Peter Gorman at his home in Joshua. I immediately accepted the opportunity.

At the time, I was renting a room in Garland while working as a car salesman at a Chevrolet dealership in Dallas. It was one of the dealerships that had commercials and billboards scattered all over the place, as well as spots on all the local news programs. I had previous experience selling advertising to car dealerships, but I had never worked at a car dealership as an employee. I ended up selling Chevys because I was in desperate need of a job. I didn't have the luxury of time to send out resumes or elaborate on how I had spent the past three years living out in the woods. I found out that I was actually pretty good at selling cars. The selling was the easy part. Waiting around for customers to show up at a car dealership in the scorching heat of a Texas summer is an experience that I wouldn't wish upon my worst enemy. It was also pure hell trying to earn an honest living in a building full of crooks, most of whom were high on cocaine. I did manage to make some money as a car salesman, and after a few weeks of sleeping in my car, I was able to rent a room.

The Peter Gorman interview was being recorded for Lorenzo Hagerty, and his Psychedelic Salon podcast. I had been listening to the Psychedelic Salon for several years, so I was excited to be a part of this recording. I met George in Arlington, and from there we drove to Fort Worth to pick up Tom, and continued on to Joshua. A few years prior, George and Tom had interviewed Lorenzo at his home in southern California for a documentary film project about the Starck Club in Dallas. This interview was eventually turned into a short film called *Confessions of an Ecstasy Advocate*. During the car ride to Joshua, Tom made a call to Lorenzo, and I could hear Lorenzo's voice coming through Tom's phone. It felt surreal to be a part of this recording of psychedelic history.

This was my second visit to Gorman's house, and his office still left me in awe. We interviewed Peter for over four hours that day, and he was at the top of his storytelling game. He told story after story about traveling to Peru, and visiting indigenous tribes. He went into vivid details about doing sapo with his teacher Pablo. He talked about hunting with the Matses, and taking a riverboat up the Javary River on the border of Peru and Brazil. He told the story about how he met, and fell in love with his ex-wife Chepa, after hiring her to captain his boat up the Javary. We interviewed

Chepa as well, and she talked about meeting Dr. Richard Evans Schultes at Harvard when Peter worked for *High Times*. Chepa also told us the story about how she met Peter on the boulevard in Iquitos. She said that she thought Peter talked too much, but he was a very good dancer.

One of the stories Peter told us that day was how he became the first non-indigenous person to have a sapo experience, and publish about the experience. This man from Queens had more stories than anyone I had ever met. Throughout the interview, he chain smoked one cigarette after another. It was like interviewing Charles Bukowski, Hunter S. Thompson, and Richard Evans Schultes all in one afternoon. We had three cameras set up that day, and I operated one of them. I was soaking up all of these jungle stories, and imaging what it must have been like to see the Matses back in the mid 80s. The audio recording from that day ended up being played in two parts on the Psychedelic Salon podcast, episodes #467 and #468. It was during this interview that I became convinced that I needed to go to Peru to make a film about Peter Gorman.

Later that evening Peter hosted a sapo session. This was my initial encounter with sapo. I had been surrounded by frogs my whole life, but I didn't know much about them. I didn't know anything about the giant monkey tree frog, and I had no idea what to expect from sapo. I hadn't even read Peter's book, *Sapo in My Soul*, and I was feeling a little anxious. Well, to be completely honest, I was actually extremely nervous. At five-thirty, my friends from the Love Tribe arrived for the sapo session. The Love Tribe was a group of people from across North Texas who introduced me to ayahuasca, so I trusted them when they spoke very highly of sapo. There were nine of us that day for the sapo session. Everyone paid fifty bucks to receive sapo.

Peter had a helper for the sapo session, his friend Hector from Switzerland. Hector helped run Peter's website, and was the person who found the tape with the recording of Peter's interview with Dr. Albert Hofmann from 1993 when Peter worked for *High Times*. The recording was an interview where Dr. Hofmann thought he was talking to *Time* magazine, so he tried to negotiate a fee for his participation in the interview. After Hector found the recording in Peter's garage, he sent it to Lorenzo, and it became podcast #280. The rediscovery of that recording with Dr. Hofmann is what led us to Peter's house for a follow-up interview.

Peter sat at the front of the room chain-smoking Camel cigarettes, while everyone gathered in the living room. He spoke to the group about sapo, and what they could expect during the experience. He had changed his shirt since the interview, and slicked back his hair. Peter addressed the group with the sharpness of a college professor. While Peter was talking, I couldn't stop staring at the flesh eating bacteria scars on his legs. I would not find out until later the whole story about the legs. I wasn't sure that Peter was healthy enough to administer medicine to anyone, but I wasn't backing out.

I had a crush on this woman sitting next to me, and I didn't want her thinking that I was scared of a little frog medicine. Peter had each of the participants roll up their sleeves, so the medicine could be applied on the upper part of our arms. One at a time, the participants knelt at Peter's computer desk, and waited for him to burn them with the tamishi. Peter heated up the tamishi using a cigarette lighter until it was red hot. Peter was known to use really large pieces of tamishi. The tamishi vine can be different sizes, but commonly it is about the same diameter as the tip of a match.

Peter asked each person, "How many do want, and where do you want 'em?" Most of the group received two or three dots. One guy asked for five. Peter smiled and said, "How about three? This is some strong fucking medicine man! Straight from the Matses. Just got it three days ago. I sneezed my ass off when I opened it up, so that means this is a strong motherfucker!"

Peter sat at his small computer desk, and prepared his sapo stick. He used an expensive chef's knife (cost him $2000 according to Peter) to scrap the dried secretion off the stick. He carefully mixed the secretion into the saliva, creating a paste. There was a method to doing this, and you could tell that Peter had been working with sapo for a very long time. It required a significant amount of time, energy, and saliva to administer sapo to nine people. Peter explained that after eleven minutes, his daughter Madelaina would remove the sapo from our arm. Peter informed us that he would sing at the beginning of the session. He explained, "I sing to calm people, and to bring the energy down after a group has received sapo. Even though the singing is not traditional, I have found that the singing works really well with sapo. The Matses that I met did not sing or play any kind of instruments during sapo sessions. Sapo was just a part of life. They would do it whenever, and wherever they needed to do it. They would just look at you, and laugh at your pain, and they wouldn't sing you any songs."

After Peter had the sapo ready, he invited each person to come back up to his computer desk to be served. Each person knelt down as before, and Peter applied the sapo. I received two dots of sapo on my arm. Peter started singing in Spanish, and I had never heard anything quite like it before. I had heard some people sing in ayahuasca circles, but Peter's singing was unlike anything I had heard before. I didn't understand a word of it, but his song set the perfect tone for the session.

About a minute into the sapo experience I wasn't feeling much. Then two minutes in, I started to feel really hot. At the five minute mark, I started thinking, "Why the hell did I do this?" Ten minutes passed, and I felt like I was dying. I felt miserable, and I really wanted to fight Gorman for making me feel this bad. I remember thinking that I was never, doing it again. My stomach was twisted in knots. I felt as though a vise grip had been clamped down on my insides, squeezing tightly. I desperately wanted it to be over. The operatic sounds of projectile vomiting into plastic buckets filled the room. I felt like I was in that scene in *Stand By Me*, where everyone was puking.

Peter sat calmly in his rocking chair smoking a cigarette, watching over the room like a hawk. This medicine was strong. This was serious medicine. I didn't vomit, but I certainly felt like I was on the verge. Several people in the group had their faces swell.

The peak pain time was probably only five minutes or so, but it felt like an hour. Peter's daughter Madelaina came by, and wiped the sapo off my arm. This let me know that the worst of it was over. The pain and agony began to fade after Gorman announced that it had been fifteen minutes. He said that we should start feeling like we are coming back into our bodies. Suddenly, I could hear better, and I could smell like a bloodhound. The pain had completely left my body. I noticed that my vision was clear and sharp. I felt energized and strong. The medicine had been rough for a few individuals, but everyone ended up with a good sapo experience that evening at Gorman's.

After the sapo, Peter offered the jungle snuff called nunu to anyone who wanted it. Several in the group took him up on the offer, but I declined. Peter administered the nunu by blowing the green powder up the nostrils through a hollow jungle reed. A couple of people in the group had a more intense experience with the nunu, than they did with the sapo. I was glad that I had passed on the nunu.

September 22, 2015 - Jack County, Texas

This was the three year anniversary of the last time I got drunk. It's an easy day to remember because my Dad's birthday is September 22, and it's also the birthday of my best friend Dirk Leatherwood. After getting blackout drunk, and cussing out my family on my Dad's 70th birthday, I knew I needed a change. A couple of weeks later, a childhood friend of mine asked me if I wanted to take magic mushrooms. I had not experienced any psychedelic mushrooms since my college days in San Marcos. This was my first experience with magic mushrooms without the added element of heavy drinking. I had been listening to a lot of Terence McKenna lectures, so I was very much on board with expanding my reality. I had wanted to do a mushroom trip ever since I had watched the documentary *American: The Bill Hicks Story, a*nd heard how mushrooms changed Bill's life.

I didn't opt for a heroic dose as McKenna recommended, but I did brew a tea using Syrian rue seeds, and consumed the tea about a half an hour before ingesting the mushrooms. I had read in McKenna's book *Food of the Gods* that Syrian rue (Peganum harmala) in combination with psilocybin in any form would enhance the effects of psilocybin.

I consumed only two grams of mushrooms, but combined with the Syrian rue tea, it was potent enough to help end seventeen years of hardcore alcoholism. While I didn't witness any hallucinations, a clear inner voice spoke to me during the experience. The voice conveyed to me that alcohol was the root cause of all my problems, revealing that I had been an alcoholic my entire adult life, and that it was time to leave that chapter behind. For the first time in my adult life, I was able to break free from the alcoholism that had plagued me since I graduated high school. The experience had left me feeling revitalized, and provided me with much needed inspiration during a time when I desperately needed it.

My nickname in college at Texas State (then called Southwest Texas State) was McKenna, but it had nothing to do with Terence McKenna. They called me McKenna, because one night in 1996 I drank a fifth of Henry McKenna whiskey in less than an hour, and almost died of alcohol poisoning. It was not a hazing incident, but this was an episode of "ritualized drinking" for new members of a fraternity that I had joined. It was Big Brother Night, and all the new members had to buy a bottle of Henry McKenna bourbon to drink with their Big Brother. I had almost drank the entire bottle before my Big Brother had even arrived. It was my own foolishness and insecurity that led me to drink the whole bottle. Fortunately, a guy named Dave stuck his finger down my throat, and made me vomit, saving my life. I don't remember any of this, but was later informed that this had occurred. I never did thank Dave, but I did try to fight him a couple of times after that night. I'm not sure why, but maybe I was mad at him because he didn't let me die that night. Thank you Dave for not letting me die.

I was grateful to have made it three years without getting drunk. I knew how lucky I was. My Mom told me that she was very proud of the positive changes that she had seen in my behavior since that time when the Dallas police called, and woke her up. The Dallas police informed her that they had found me passed out on a sidewalk in downtown Dallas, and they were escorting me to jail. Apparently, I had drank too much free booze at the Dallas Film Festival.

I was ready to direct my first movie, and everything was lining up for me to be in Peru shooting a documentary in January. I had always wanted to go to South America, and now I had the perfect tour guide.

6
FROM QUIET DESPERATION TO EXTRAORDINARY

Adventures only happen to those incapable of planning an expedition.
- Richard Evans Schultes

Most men lead lives of quiet desperation. These people don't want to be desperate. They want to do something extraordinary.
- Peter Gorman

November 21, 2015 - Joshua, Texas

I finally made the decision that I was going to Peru to make the documentary about Gorman. Originally, there were plans for me to be a co-director along with my friends George and Tom. However, we had disagreements over the direction of the film. They didn't believe that we had to go Peru to make the film, but I insisted that there would be no film, if we didn't go to Peru to shoot it. So, I decided to direct it alone, and I was determined to film

Peter's trip in January. I drove down to Joshua to pay him a deposit for his jungle jaunt, and arrived at Peter's place at three-thirty on a beautiful Saturday afternoon. I sat, and listened to Peter talk for hours about his adventures in the Amazon, and his work with the Matses. I asked a few questions, but Peter did most of the talking. He told me stories about the Rio Galvez, and going up the Javary in a riverboat. He said there were caimans as far as the eye could see on the Rio Galvez. He had stories about how they encountered Hasidic Jews growing marijuana on the Amazon River, and he said they stopped at a leper colony on their way to visit the Matses. On that same trip river pirates tried to take over his boat. One story he told me is also in his book, *Sapo in My Soul*. It's the story of watching a woman nursing a baby monkey, while the mother was roasted over a campfire. Gorman's jungle stories almost always included snakes and guns. He loved telling stories that involved certain elements of danger. His stories were often jaw dropping, and graphic, but they were oddly comforting in the way that Peter told them.

After an hour full of jungle stories, I finally gathered the courage to ask Peter if he had any sapo and nunu. Of course he did, and he quickly pulled out his sapo stick and started to prepare his jungle medicine. Gorman took a piece of tamashi, and lit one end of it with a cigarette lighter. He gave me three burns on my upper arm. He filled the burns with large dots of sapo. Then he shook his chakapa, and sang in Spanish for several minutes.

I didn't sweat as much as the first time, but I did get very nauseous for fifteen minutes. My stomach felt like it was twisting in knots. My head got very hot, and for a short time it seemed like my head was suspended above my body. Fifteen minutes felt like an hour. This experience was intense, and I could hear my insides making noises. This second session with sapo I learned that three dots was a large dose, and it was a big step up from two dots.

Peter offered me nunu after the sapo session, and I needed it this time. I had been dealing with a severe sinus infection, and had tried several herbal remedies, but nothing seemed to work. I had turned down nunu after my first sapo session last summer, but not this time. I was a little intimidated with nunu, because of what I had witnessed this jungle snuff do the last time I was at Gorman's. Also, I was a bit concerned about my past. I used to put a lot of substances up my nose like cocaine, adderall, and ecstasy, and I didn't like the idea of snorting powder again. There was a time in my life when some people referred to me as the cocaine cowboy.

My thoughts on tobacco before I met Peter Gorman was that tobacco had no purpose other than to harm people. I had witnessed many family members die from lung cancer after years of smoking American cigarettes. Even though I knew that tobacco was considered a master teacher plant, I didn't fully grasp how this could be possible, until I smoked a South American mapacho, and experienced Amazonian jungle snuffs. Terence McKenna wrote in his book *Food of the Gods* that mapacho is "much more potent, chemically complex, and potentially hallucinogenic than the commercial grades of Nicotiana tabacum available today. Tobacco was and is the ever-present adjunct of the more powerful and visionary hallucinogenic plants wherever in the Americas they are used in a traditional and shamanic way."

Notes from my first nunu experience:

When the first dose of nunu was blown up my nostrils, it felt like someone had ignited gun powder in my nose, and punched me in the back of my head. The intensity almost knocked me down. The second nostril was just as bad as the first. I was in extreme pain. My head was spinning. My eyes watered, and I felt very sick. I was done after the first one, but Peter said I had to have three doses in each nostril. "What-the-fuck?" was going through my head. He promised that the second, and third blows wouldn't feel like the first one did, and it didn't. I held the nunu for a short time before my nasal cavities cleared, and suddenly dark liquids gushed out of my nose. The plastic bag was not big enough, and fluids spilled out on Peter's living room floor. It was pretty nasty, and I kept apologizing to Peter as I was cleaning up the mess with paper towels. But it was no big deal to Peter, he had seen much worse, and I wasn't the first person to vomit on his living room floor. The nunu had completely cleared up my sinus infection, and I was certain that I would never try nunu again.

December 27, 2015 - Joshua, Texas

This was the first day of shooting any footage for the documentary. Once I had committed to making the film, I had a tough time deciding what camera to use in the jungle. I couldn't afford to buy a camera, and I couldn't afford to pay a professional cinematographer to come along on the trip. One day when visiting with George Wada he told me that I should just shoot the film on my Samsung Galaxy. George was a technical genius, and a wonderful photographer, and filmmaker that I had known for almost ten years. Initially, I resisted George's suggestion, because I wanted the film to have a professional look. I had seen some bad independent films shot on cellphones, and

I didn't want the label of a cellphone movie. Then I remembered that L.M. Kit Carson had made a documentary series called *Africa Diary* with a Nokia N93 cellphone back in 2006. I had met Kit through his son Hunter, when Kit was living in Dallas, and working on post-production for *Africa Diary*. I consider Kit to be a mentor of mine, and one of the biggest inspirations for me going to South America to make a documentary. When making *Africa Diary*, Kit had visited three countries: Mozambique, South Africa, and Zambia, and he did short segments with narration on each country. Kit was in Africa because he had been hired by what he described as, "first-timer wealthy do-gooder doc-makers as consultant for a documentary that they are going to shoot in Mozambique, Africa." Kit had experience in North Africa, because he had traveled there doing Sundance story writing workshops.

Kit wanted to shoot some footage on his own while in Africa helping the do-gooders, and he wanted a camera that would not bring attention to his effort. He needed something that would blend in to the environment, and not cause the "uh-oh, I'm on camera" veil to go up between the shooter and the subject. He wanted a fly-on-the-wall approach, not a seven-man film crew like the do-gooders. Kit studied all the Sony/Red Camera/Flip Cams/Mini-Cams that were available at the time, and nothing seemed to be right until a friend of his told him about the Nokia N93. That friend was a cinematographer named Ueli Steiger, who had worked on Roland Emmerich's films. Kit picked up a N93 on his way to LAX to catch his twenty-two hour flight to Monzambique.

When Kit came back from Africa he put together a DVD of what he had shot, and sent it to Robert Redford for his birthday. Redford loved the footage, and set up a meeting in New York City with five executives from the Sundance Channel. Kit showed the executives what he had been shooting on his cellphone, and some of them were crying by the end of the screening. One of the executives turned to Kit, "Okay what do you want to do?".

Kit replied, "I want to go back." Kit made a deal with the Sundance executives, and he went back to Africa. He spent four months in each country shooting on his cell-phone, and every night he would download the footage that he shot to his Macbook.

After my conversation with George, I started looking at footage shot by my Samsung Galaxy, and I was convinced that maybe George was on to something. This phone had the ability to shoot in 4k. The technology had advanced a lot in the years since Kit had made *Africa Diary*.

The Love Tribe had planned another trip to Gorman's for a sapo session, and I thought this would be a great opportunity to test out my camera before I left for Peru. When I arrived at Peter's that day I was a little nervous about shooting during a sapo session. This was my first documentary, and I was a one-man crew. Ten people attended the session that day, and I was good friends with most of the group. Before the session I announced to the group that I was making a documentary about Peter. Kit was right about the cellphone not giving off that "uh-oh I'm on camera" feeling. And I focused on shots of Peter, not the participants of the session. I used the fly-on-the-wall approach like Kit used. I couldn't believe that I was actually making a movie. I felt a lot of gratitude for being present to record that sapo session that day at Peter Gorman's house.

Madeleina made sure that everyone had their sleeves rolled up properly so their sleeves wouldn't fall down, and knock the secretion off their arms. Peter burned the guests with the tamishi vine one at a time. After everyone had they burn marks, Peter began applying the sapo, and as soon as everyone had been served, Peter began singing an icaro. Almost immediately after Peter started singing, Madeleina had to help walk a couple of people to the bathroom. It was a major cleansing for this group. The synchronized sounds of vomiting created an almost orchestrated purge, with a strangely rhythmic tone. Madeleina passed out moistened paper towels to cool off the guests. Several women purged in buckets, while Madaleina held their hair. It was beautiful to watch the teamwork of Peter and Madeleina. The more I watched, the more I realized that Madeleina had been doing this type of medicine work her whole life, and Peter had taught her very well. You could tell that Peter was very proud of his daughter, and her ability to facilitate a sapo session. The test shoot with the cellphone was a success. I had a camera. I shot a lot of footage that day, and some of it ended up in the film. It truly captured the essence of a Sunday afternoon at the Gorman's house.

In the film, I aimed to showcase the stark contrast between Peter's life in Texas, and his life in Peru. My idea for the film was inspired by the documentary *The American Dreamer,* and the allure of being present at Dennis Hopper's house in Taos in 1970. *The American Dreamer* is a 1971 Dennis Hopper documentary, co-directed by L.M. Kit Carson and Larry Schiller. *The American Dreamer* was shot mostly in Taos, New Mexico in 1970 at Dennis Hopper's home, a twenty-two room adobe house once owned by Mabel Dodge Luhan. During the making of the docucmentary, Hopper was in the middle of post production on a film that he shot in Chinchero, Peru called *The Last Movie*. This was Hopper's follow-up to *Easy Rider*. *The Last Movie* won Best Feature at the Venice Film Festival in 1971, and Hopper had declared it, "the first American art film." The studio hated *The Last Movie*, mainly because it went over budget, and the experimentally editing took sixteen months to finish. *The Last Movie* opened in one theater in New York City in September of 1971, and broke the theater's single-day ticket sales record, but the film was pulled from the theater after only two weeks. It was a movie that went mostly unseen for fifty years until it was digitally restored in 2018.

January 8, 2016 - Iquitos, Peru

I had left for Peru for the first time on January 2, 2016. My parents thought I had lost my mind. I didn't exactly inherit the travel bug. My Dad had never be on an airplane, and my Mom hadn't been in an airplane since the early seventies. Neither one of them had been outside the United States. The year prior to the trip, I had been struggling to pay my phone bill, which left my parents baffled as to how I had scraped together enough money to travel to South America to make a movie. I had secured a job as a closer on real estate transactions that helped buyers and sellers sign banking and mortgage documents. It worked out great, because January was a slow month for closings, and this allowed me to take some extended time away from work.

After spending six days in Iquitos, this place felt like a different planet. I was completely taken aback by the unparalleled beauty, and unfamiliarity of this place. It was unlike any place I had ever seen. The weather was scorching hot, but the daily rain showers provided a much needed relief from the intense heat. The South American summer weather was a welcome change from the bitter winter conditions I had left behind in Texas.

I had just turned forty the previous week, and reaching Amazonia felt like a significant milestone in my life. I had read somewhere that women greatly outnumbered the men in Peru, and based on my early observations, I believed this to be true. I regretted not learning more Spanish before the trip. Beautiful Peruvian women seemed to be everywhere I turned, yet I found myself unable to communicate with most of them.

Iquitos is known as the "Capital of the Peruvian Amazon", and is located at the meeting of three rivers: Amazon, Itaya, and Nanay. Iquitos reminded me of a town that you might see in an Alejandro Jodorowsky film, or read about in a Philip K. Dick book. Iquitos is undeniably one of the most captivating, and unique places that I'd ever had the privilege of exploring. As I walked around the streets of Iquitos I watched men juggle machetes in the street for money, while motorcycles flew past me with babies hanging off the back of their mother.

I found it fascinating that Iquitos is the largest city in the world that could not be accessed by road. It is only accessible by boat or plane. The area around Iquitos was home to many indigenous peoples, before being founded as a city in 1757 by Spanish Jesuits. During the late 1800s Iquitos became the center of export for the Amazon rubber boom. Iquitos today is still considered the gateway to Amazonia, and the beginning of the Amazon River. There are very few automobiles in Iquitos, and the most common mode of transportation to get around the city is motorcars, which are motorcycles with a cage welded to the back with seats for passengers. It is a very cheap way to get around town, and there are motorcars everywhere you turn in Iquitos.

I woke up early so I could walk down to the boulevard, and capture footage of the Amazon River at sunrise. There is nothing quite like witnessing a sunrise deep in the heart of Amazonia. I enjoyed breakfast at Fitzcarraldo's, a restaurant on the boulevard that has posters, photographs, and memorabilia from Werner Herzog's 1982 film. The walls are covered with items from the making of *Fitzcarraldo*.

It's a wonderful place to begin your day as a filmmaker. When you are surrounded by reminders of Herzog's masterpiece, any filmmaker would feel a surge of creativity and inspiration to bring their own artistic vision to life. I could see why Herzog was captivated by Iquitos, and it was inspiring to be walking the same streets as Herzog and Klaus Kinski did when making *Fitzcarraldo*. Iquitos had managed to retain its unpredictable charm. The bustling markets, the vibrant street life, and the constant buzz of the motorcars all remained unchanged. The colonial buildings erected during the rubber boom still adorned the streets. However, noticeable changes had taken place as the city had evolved, and become more modernized over the last thirty years, but the spirit of this jungle town endured, and it remained untamed, and full of surprises. Fitzcarraldo tells the story of an Irishman who dreams of bringing an opera house to Iquitos. I felt the spirit of this character throughout my time in Iquitos, inspiring me to create my own film about an Irishman.

Iquitos, January 17, 1981

**Shooting. The strike is on again in the city, but none of this seems as bad as the feverish horrors the rumors had projected. The water rose so high that it came in through the floor of my cabin. A pillow was floating around. In the morning, when I put on my pants they felt cold and odd. I turned one pant leg inside out, and a frog jumped out."
- Werner Herzog, *Conquest of the Useless: Reflections From The Making of Fitzcarraldo***

Today was the first day of Peter's trip, and we met at his office, La Noche, a restaurant on the boulevard. Peter was good friends with the owner of La Noche, and had been using the restaurant as his office/base camp for many years. Peter had a designated chair at La Noche whenever he was in town. It's where Peter conducted his business meetings, and if Peter was in Iquitos, you could always find him at La Noche. Peter's trips began with the first two days purchasing the necessary supplies, and getting outfitted with jungle gear. Peter's trips typically included six to twelve people from various corners of the globe, each bringing a unique perspective, and life experience to the journey. Some of his guests were very experienced with jungle medicines, and some had no experience at all.

Peter wanted his guests spending a couple of days together in Iquitos, so they could get to know the other guests, and become more comfortable with Peter and his team. The goal was to build a level of trust before getting to the jungle. There were eight of us on this jungle jaunt. The group included me, a lawyer from Austin, two sisters from California, an eighty-three year old retiree from Minnesota and his forty-something-year-old divorced son, and an expat in his forties accompanied by a much older Danish woman. I'm not sure of the relationship between the expat and the Danish woman, and I didn't bother to ask.

We were all seated, and patiently waiting for Peter's instructions. "I didn't discover frog sweat," Peter told the group. "But I happen to be the first gringo who took it, and then wrote about it. That we know of. Somebody else might've done it before me, but they didn't publish it. Or if they did, it's obscure, and nobody can find it." Peter lit a cigarette, and took a swig from his glass of aguardiente. There was loud Peruvian music playing in the background. "From Peru comes the world's supply of tomatoes, the world's supply of potatoes. There was a yam in Africa, and a sweet potato in Mexico, but the other fourteen hundred varieties are from Peru. Peanuts are from here as well," says Peter. Peter continued to captivate the group with stories about wondering through Amazonia with his jungle guide, Moises Vienna Torress. He mentioned that one of the few rules on the trip was a strict prohibition against cocaine. He emphasized that anyone caught with cocaine, or using cocaine would be immediately removed from the trip, no questions asked. I was relieved that my cocaine days was a thing of the past. "My litmus test is tell me the names of three or four of the rains here. Well you got, lluvia loca. Lluvia is rain. Loca is crazy. But what it means is crazy girl rain. It's like a teenage girl who bounces from one to the next, and can't make up her mind. So that's the rain that might start coming in this way, and three minutes later the wind is blowing in the opposite direction. And then two minutes later, it's coming down as hail. Loca, it's crazy rain. Then you borracho, a thunder lightening storm, and the significance is that it's like when your dad comes home dead drunk, and says where's my family, what's going on here! He starts screaming, and he kicks a chair, and yells get out of here kids! Don't worry it's gonna pass. Two minutes later, he's gonna fall asleep. So you're fine with that one. Then you got tampesto. And tampesto is a rain that's a thunder lightening storm for twelve freakin' hours. It's your mother and dad fighting, irreconcilably, kids just hide under the bed, 'cause they're gonna take it out on you too. Tampesto is a tough rain. And then you got warmi llueva. Warmi means woman in Quecha.

Warmi llueva significance is that it's a little drizzle. It goes on and on, so it's a bitchy woman rain. She's not gonna kill ya, but she's just not going to let you go. She's going to pick at you until you go nuts. Those are four of them for instance, there are more."

After an hour of sorting out the bill, we headed off in motorcars for the Belen market. Those who have spent time in Iquitos will understand what I mean by "sorting out the bill". In Iquitos, it seems that you always end up paying for something that you did not order.

Peter had a team of six to eight Peruvians on his trips. The team handled all the luggage, and escorted Peter's guests around Iquitos. The larger the group meant the larger the team. The team was made up of family members of Peter's teacher, Julio Jerena. Peter first met Julio in 1985 when Peter's guide Moises Torres Vienna took him to Julio's land, two-hundred twelve kilometers south of Iquitos. The camp where Peter hosted his jungle trips was Julio's ancestral home on the Aucayau River. The land now belonged to Julio's daughter Lady, and her husband Juan. Lady and Juan's children were members of Peter's team: George, Jherman, Kaye, Ruber, Sidalith. They had been working with Peter since they were children, and have known Peter their whole lives. The curandero for the trip was Julio's son, Jairo. He would be serving the ayahausca in a couple of nights.

Peter always arranged a trip to the Belen Market to provide his guests with a glimpse of Peruvian culture. Belen boasted a diverse array of exotic fruits, vegetables, and odd-looking fish and meat. Everywhere you turned there were apples, avocados, bananas, cantaloupes, cucumbers, grapes, mangos, watermelons, and numerous other Amazonian fruits and vegetables that I couldn't identify. The produce was sourced from farms located all along the Amazon River basin. The market was bustling with activity, and Peter warned us to stick together as a group to ensure our safety, and to prevent any potential theft from pickpockets.

I followed Peter down Medicine Alley as he was greeted by the vendors selling their jungle medicines. He walked over to a booth where a woman hugged him, and offered him a chair to sit. The woman and Peter had been friends for many years, and Peter always took his guests to see her when they visited Belen. The woman pulled out a cup, and poured Peter one of her magical root potions. She proceeded to distribute a cup to each guest, and poured out a dark liquid from a bottle labeled "7 Roots." I found out later that "7 Roots" was generally sold as an aphrodisiac. The majority of the remedies, and potions available for purchase at the Belen market are promoted as aphrodisiacs, appealing to tourists seeking to enhance their romantic escapades. I bought a bottle just in case it worked. The woman handed Peter a package of bark labeled "Una de Gato (cat's claw)", and the bulb of a plant called sacha jergon.

Peter began his lecture, "Jergons are a whole group of poisonous pit vipers down here, and we call them jergons. Sacha jergon, one single flower comes up like this, and leans over, and its bright red on its face. Then you dig down, and you find its coiled body, like a snake. But this (pointing to sacha jergon) is one of the best darn tumor reducers. It's being used as adjunct therapy in lots, and lots of hospitals around the world. Hospitals can't get it for you, but they say I would recommend that you might send somebody out for some cat's claw and sacha jergon. Because these two together will boost your immune system, twenty, thirty, fifty points a day in the first two weeks."

I asked, "How do you consume these two?"

Peter responded, "You take two of these sticks, and you twist them and crack them, and split them into four or five smaller pieces. Put them in three liters of water. Steep it. And over the course of twelve hours it reduces from three liters to one liter. At that point strain it. And drink three-fourths of an ounce in the morning, and one at night. In the last hour of cooking the una de gato, you can add the powder of the sacha jergon."

The market was bustling with noise, and we found ourselves standing in the middle of the lively aisle, fully engaged in Peter's words. I had my phone positioned close, but I wasn't sure if the audio would be clear enough to use. The visuals were striking, yet I was uncertain about the sound quality captured. "Usually I do it, and I recommend that my family do it, and people who call me and ask me for help. I recommend just make the liter. The liter will last three weeks, more or less. Then take a week off. You don't want your body totally dependent on anything," said Peter as he smiled, and turned to answer questions from the group.

"Do you have powder?", the lawyer asked the woman. The lawyer and I both purchased several bags of cat's claw bark, and sacha jergon powder.

Peter seemed to thrive on the chaos of Belen. You can could find just about anything you wanted in Belen, if you talked to the right person. "You want ayahuasca? No Problem. You want huachuma? No problem. You want coca? No problem, " boasted a Medicine Alley vendor.

As we wandered through the meat market section of Belen, Peter shared stories of what the market was like in 1984, when he first arrived in Peru. I was mesmerized by all the exotic fish, and there was many different species of fish that I didn't recognize. I had never seen so many different cuts of turtle meat in my life; apparently, turtle meat was in high demand here. I recommend going to Belen early in morning before the smell of rotted meat fills the air later in the day. As we exited the meat section, Dozens of vultures were perched up on the power lines above the market. They were poised to swoop down on any meat that might be dropped on the ground. I bought a roll of mapachos for the journey to the jungle, and a couple of bottles of Agua de Florida (cologne) as we left Belen. I returned to the hotel to drop off the items I purchased at Belen, and took a motorcar to La Casa Fitzcarraldo, a hotel near the port.

It was just a five-minute ride from the Plaza de Armas. This hotel served as the base camp hotel for the production for two Werner Herzog's films: *Aguirre, The Wrath of God* (1972) and *Fitzcarraldo* (1982). Mick Jagger stayed here when he was working on *Fitzcarraldo*, as did the two stars of the film, Klaus Kinski and Claudia Cardinale. One hundred foot tall trees, and plants surrounded the pool, which was not crowded, because they charged a cover to walk through the door. The solitude was well worth the fifteen soles they charged for admission. I enjoyed a nice Peruvian breakfast by the pool, while sitting across from a large mural of Klaus Kinski that was painted on the wall.

After a few hours relaxing by the pool, I went back to La Noche to catch back up with the group. Peter was holding court, and telling stories about walking across Amazonia, when someone asked him about the bright yellow charapita pepper that Peru is famous for. Peter smiled and replied, "They are quite hot, there not ghost peppers or anything, but they are quite hot. But they're so little, that you just to tend to, when you first see them to pop a couple in your mouth. The big river turtle is also called the charapita, and then the women here are called charapitas as well. What they have in common is this. When you eat those hot peppers the first time, you might just have a handful. You will probably never do that again. They're just too goddamn hot. The big river turtle has no mating season, and will mate with any male, anytime, once. If he comes back she will just tear him to pieces. And the women here are pretty much like that. They will be as hot as you can be, once. God forbid you ever come back. You're a notch on their belt, not vice versa. Those are the three charapitas. Cautionary note, don't go back for seconds."

Later that evening, I met some American guys in their twenties from Pennsylvania. They had been enjoying the party scene in Iquitos, and discovered the consequences of venturing into places where gringos did not belong. The night before, one of them had been mugged, robbed, and left naked on the outskirts of Iquitos. Somebody spiked his drink, causing him to blackout. The thieves beat the shit out of him, and stole all of his belongings, including his passport. He was lucky to be alive. The Americans seemed a bit shaken by the incident, and this made me contemplate what could have happened, if I had visited Iquitos in my twenties. Crime and robbery are major issues in Iquitos due to the city's economic disparities, and the lack of opportunities for many of its residents. Crime is a means of survival. Peter always said that Iquitos was home to some of the best thieves in the world, and it can be dangerous for the unsuspecting tourist, especially after dark. I cautioned those young Americans to be careful, but I know how I ignored warnings in my twenties.

Peter arranged for his team to take the group to check out the most popular band in Iquitos, Explosion. The band Explosion is known for making their own versions of native songs and stories. The group was created in 1998 by Raul Flores, who started the group with three components for guaranteed success: 1) Get a really good sound system 2) Hire beautiful female dancers 3) Hire the best ensemble of vocalists, and musicians that you can find. Flores sold his investors by telling them that if he had all three of these components, huge crowds would show up, and they did.

Attending my first Explosion show was a concert experience that I will never forget. There were fifteen hundred Peruvians crammed into this large amphitheater, and at the back of the amphitheater there was a soccer complex with kids practicing soccer. We bought a couple of Cristal beers, and walked up a flight of stairs to get a better view of the band. The scantily clad dancers rotated in groups of six every couple of songs. I found myself daydreaming about these stunning Amazonian women. It was hard to pay attention to the music, when the dancers were so enchanting. The crowd knew every word, and sang along the entire show. Explosion was a well-oiled machine that brought in huge crowds four nights a week. They must have had ten lead singers. I didn't understand the words to their songs, but I loved the way their music made the crowd feel. It made me feel closer to Iquitos. I was grateful to have witnessed their electrifying live performance. This band was a big part of the musical landscape in Iquitos, and if you walk around town, you will hear Explosion echoing from restaurants, shops, and on radios being carried on motorcars.

7
Julio's Place

If I'm an advocate for anything, it's to move. As far as you can, as much as you can. Across the ocean, or simply across the river. The extent to which you can walk in someone else's shoes or at least eat their food, it's a plus for everybody. Open your mind, get off the couch, move.
- Anthony Bourdain

January 10, 2016 - Iquitos, Peru

I had spent a week in Iquitos, and I was ready to get the hell out of this town. The novelty of Iquitos had worn off. I had my fair share of Peruvian nightlife, and my tolerance for the street hustlers, and the ayahuasca peddlers had reached its limit. Peter's group had split into two parts. I'm not sure what the other four guests were doing, but our group of four was having a blast exploring Iquitos, and immersing ourselves in the Peruvian culture. We were enjoying the three Peruvian soles for one U.S. Dollar conversion, and living like kings. We ate lots of delicious Peruvian food, dishes like aji de gallina, anticuchos de corrosion, lomo saltado, papas a la huancaina, and pollo a la brasa. We did all the tourist activities like going to Monkey Island, and the Pilpintuwasi Butterfly Farm. Everything seemed so affordable, and soles were flowing like Monopoly money.

I began to notice that I was going through soles rather quickly because the street hustlers were on every corner, attempting to lure you into a deal for a jaguar claw necklace, or an anaconda bracelet adorned with amethyst and ayahuasca vine. Selling homemade jewelry to tourists is a significant part of the economy in Iquitos, and highly competitive. Learning how to politely say no is a skill that you need to practice before visiting Iquitos. Peter advised us to say, "maybe tomorrow" instead of simply saying no, and walking away. The belief in the evil eye is prevalent here, so it is best to not take any chances by pissing off the locals. During our time in Iquitos, we had unknowingly amassed quite an entourage, possibly because the lawyer had been enthusiastically buying everything that was offered to him. It felt like wherever we went, we were constantly buying beers for large groups of locals. In Peru, most beer is purchased in large bottles, and poured into plastic cups, and shared. The beer was cheap, so we didn't mind picking up a few rounds. The locals must have thought that we were wealthy Americans who could afford it. We had just arrived in town on an airplane from thousands of miles away, and we were there to spend thousands of dollars to experience jungle medicines.

We departed for the jungle that afternoon aboard a riverboat called the *Don Jose*. The vessel had the capacity to accommodate up to three hundred passengers. It looked just like the boat from *Fitzcarraldo*. The *Don Jose* was not just a passenger boat. In fact, the *Don Jose* made most of its money hauling cargo up and down the rivers of Northwest Amazonia. They were transporting everything imaginable on this boat. The boat was loaded with cases of beer, live chickens, jungle fruits, sacks of corn, and crates filled with various items. The ticket for the riverboat was twenty American dollars, which equaled about sixty soles at the time. When you purchased a ticket, it meant you were assigned a hammock, and that was all. The boat ride from Iquitos to Jenaro Herrera is twelve hours, possibly longer depending on the number of stops the riverboat has to make along the way. This riverboat operation was unlike any boat operation that I had seen in the United States. The *Don Jose* was very rustic, and there were no rules or regulations for boarding the boat. It was every man for himself, and this led to total chaos getting on and off the boat. One of the reasons for all of the chaos was because they loaded cargo while the passengers boarded the boat. There was no seat belts, life jackets, or anyone in charge for that matter. It was a free-for-all to find a seat. Children ran past me as I followed Peter's team to our spot on the boat.

During Gorman's trip, you stayed on the captain's deck, located on the upper level of the *Don Jose*. This section was blocked off from the rest of the passengers, and had several plastic chairs and a table. There was a couple of beds in the captain's quarters, and a toilet reserved for those on the captain's deck. The upper deck of the *Don Jose* provided the group a breathtaking view of the Amazon river. Peter announced to the group that there were loaded shotguns in the captain's quarters underneath the bed, just in case we were attacked by river pirates. Yes, there were pirates on this river, just like the ones Peter wrote about in *Ayahuasca in My Blood: 25 Years of Medicine Dreaming*. Someone on Peter's team mentioned that they had heard that a couple of trips before ours, river pirates attempted to board the *Don Jose*, but the crew fired shotguns, and kept the pirates off the boat. I was hoping that Peter was exaggerating when he talked about river pirates almost killing him.

I had been on lots of rivers in my life, but I had never seen a river as vast as the Amazon River. It seemed more like an ocean than a river. I had always considered myself more of a river guy than a lake or an ocean guy. This river was serious business. I thought the Mississippi was big, but it's nothing compared to the Rio Amazonas. The Amazon River is the widest river in the world, and during the wet season it can reach an incredible thirty miles wide in certain parts of the river. The majority of the Amazon River is 60 to 160 ft deep, but at its deepest point it is 330 ft deep. The Amazon River is the largest drainage system in the world with over 1,100 tributaries.

It felt like we were floating into a fantasy world as we drifted into the most beautiful sunset of my life. Maybe that's because a couple of hours into the trip Gorman had pulled out his secret stash of magic mushrooms. Gorman knew a guy who collected psilocybin mushrooms in Jenaro Herrera where lots of water buffalo grazed. Gorman didn't use a scale to weigh out the mushrooms that he gave his guests. He just looked at each guest for a moment, before deciding how many mushrooms he would give them. Peter served the mushrooms in pairs. He would give you six or eight or ten depending on your size, and experience with him. He might give the person a little more, if they had been on his trip before, and showed that they could handle it. Peter told the group that he used the mushrooms as an opportunity to introduce people to the jungle by building a bridge for their spirit to enter a new world.

Life is different in the jungle, and you feel it when you get there. Peter took a few mushrooms in his hand, and blew mapacho smoke on them before handing them to me. I didn't count how many he gave me. I just ate the mushrooms as fast as I could, and chased them down with water before I had a chance to taste them. It didn't take long for the mushrooms to start having an effect. I began to fade into a dreamlike state rather quickly. I felt like we had left this planet, maybe we had drifted into another dimension. The mushrooms were kicking my ass about the time the sun started going down. A thousand thoughts were running through my head all at once. I started to panic, and my heart raced. I told myself to calm down, and to focus on my breathing.

I shed tears of happiness as we floated up the Rio Ucayali. I prayed with all my heart. It was my trust in the universe that had led me here, and through will and determination I had made this journey happen. Sometimes you listen to that voice telling you to take a chance, and it turns out to be the answer that you have been searching for your whole life. The Don Jose didn't have any navigation lights; instead, they navigated the river with a spotlight attached to a broom handle. Every few minutes a man would flash the spotlight across the water to make sure that the boat was not running into objects in the river. He had a shotgun at his side in case the boat was attacked by river pirates. I had this thought that everything was alive, and everything had a purpose on this planet. Ants, bugs, mosquitos, snakes, and wasps all played a role in keeping this world going. Every moment here was like a sacred dance orchestrated by the universe. I remembered back to my childhood in the 80s, reading books that my mom had bought from a door-to-door encyclopedia salesmen. I remembered reading stories in those books about Amazonia. Those stories sparked my imagination, and fueled my curiosity about the mysteries of the rainforest, and now I was making a movie deep in the heart of Amazonia. I was a long way from Jack County.

After a few hours, the astonishment started to wear off, and I regained my composure. The riverboat kept making stop after stop, unloading and loading cargo, people, and livestock. At one of the stops, the cargaros rolled off six kegs of beer. The cargaros are the workers responsible for the loading, and unloading of cargo on the riverboat. I watched the cargaros load, and unload hundreds of sacks of rice, heavy baskets, cases of beer and sodas, and cages of chickens. One of the cargaros must have been in his seventies, but he was strong as an ox, and he wasn't wearing a shirt or any shoes. This was not an easy job, and I'm sure the pay was not that great either. I gained a lot of respect for those cargoes that night. It was a humbling experience to film those cargoes doing their job. The mushrooms had allowed me to really focus on what I was recording, and provided me an opportunity to appreciate another way of life that had existed for the last one-hundred and fifty years. The *Don Jose* must have stopped thirty times on the way to Jenaro Herrera. There were no docks at any of these stops. They simply shined a spotlight on the shore, and gently rammed the front of the boat into the riverbank. This allowed the cargoes to load, and unload cargo, and provided passengers an opportunity to jump off and on the boat.

The *Don Jose* had a small cafe where you could get food, and cervezas or Inca Colas. They served fried chicken, pork tamales, fried plantains and juane. I ordered an Inca Cola and the juane, a traditional Peruvian dish that originated in the jungle. Juane is comprised of chicken, hard-boiled eggs, olives, and rice. The rice is seasoned with cumin, oregano, turmeric, salt and pepper, and wrapped in waxy bijao leaves, and cooked. They are called jaune because they are named after the patron saint of Amazonia, San Juan (Saint John the Baptist) who was popularized in South America by Spanish missionaries. The dish is said to reference the beheading of Saint John the Baptist.

This river transportation system was a fascinating sight to witness. There were no roads or highways in this part of Amazonia. The rivers were the highways, and for a lot of Peruvian farmers and fishermen, this is the only way to get their goods to market. Riding this boat up the Rio Ucayali was an eye-opener for me. It was a lifestyle that I never knew existed before this trip. It was a life on water without automobiles. There were no paved roads just waterways. It all seemed like a better way of life. A life without being stuck in traffic, and dealing with road rage seemed refreshing to me. These river people looked happy as hell. The kids were not wearing seat belts, and nobody was freaking out about it. The stars were bright that night, and I spotted a shooting star streaking across the dark South American sky, a sign that I was headed in the right direction.

January 11, 2016 - Jenaro Herrera

We arrived at the port in Jenaro Herrerra at three a.m. It felt like we had been on the river for days. Peter's team carried our luggage as we lined up next to pallets of goods on the lower deck. I was standing next a pallet full of live chickens, and cases of Cristal beer. The riverboat slammed into the port, and people started jumping off like rats fleeing a sinking ship. It was every man, woman, and child for themselves. This method of unloading in the dark of night seemed dangerous, because the current of the Rio Ucayali is strong, and you could quickly be swept downriver if you fell off the boat. It didn't bother these river people. They had been doing these trips their whole life. It was old hat for them, and they probably could have done it blindfolded.

The streets of Jenaro Herrerra were pitch black, not a street light in sight. The headlights from a few motor cars off in the distance was all that I could see. I used my phone as a flashlight. Peter led the group through the darkness of downtown Jenaro Herrera to a small building one block from the center of town. Once inside the building, we sat down at a long table with several lit candles. The group was served cups of hot water, and Nescafe. I had grown to really like Nescafe in Peru. I'm not sure that I had even tried it back in the states. Peter began telling stories about the history of Jenaro Herrera, and how the water buffalo was first introduced to this area, making it known for its famous water buffalo cheese. The town was founded in 1954, and was named for the first lawyer in Loreto, the region in Northeast Peru where the town is located.

Peter took a drag off his Hamilton cigarette as he began his story about Jenaro Herrerra, "They wanted to bring in water buffalo, and see how water buffalo would do in this part of the jungle. Because water buffalo eat down to half of an inch from the ground, and won't mess up the ground itself, so the grass regrows. So now scientists were sent down here, and they needed assistants. They needed somebody to cook for them. They needed somebody to catch the fish, to grow the food, to cook for the scientists, and the Swedish guys. And they needed assistants to build fences for the water buffalo. And they needed some boats to move around. Everybody needed to get drunk, so they opened a small aguardiente factory. They were going to get paid, and when they got paid they wanted to get laid, so a couple of whore houses moved into town. And that opened a couple of bars for local guys. So it kind of became a boomtown. Not a boomtown like an oil town, where there was a million dollars coming through, but there was work."

I had one cup of Nescafe before I retreated to bed. It was past four a.m., and Peter was still telling stories, and entertaining the guests who couldn't sleep. Peter had reserved his guests a room at a hotel across the street from the cafe. I went to catch a couple hours of sleep, but there was a rooster nested in the rafters right next to my room, and he crowed the entire time I was trying to sleep. I decided to walk around Jernaro Herrera.

I got to the market just before sunrise, and the local farmers had just started setting up shop. There were tables selling fresh camu camu, plantains, tomatoes, yuca, and lots of other vegetables that I couldn't identify. Spiny exotic fish, and turtle parts were sold by many vendors. I saw a lot of turtle parts at the Belen market, but this small market in Jenaro Herrera seemed to have a significantly high number of turtle dealers. Outside the market there was a big radio tower next to the library. The tower had a speaker at the top with a voice making announcements in Spanish, so I didn't understand a lot of it. It reminded me of the teacher's voice in Charlie Brown. I made my way back to the small building where we had gathered the night before. I sat down, and poured myself a glass of hot water, and mixed in a couple of tablespoons of Nescafe and sugar, and a splash of milk. Peter told us that they were announcing work over the tower speaker that was available for the day. A woman brought me a hot bowl of their regional chicken soup. This chicken soup is considered one of the national dishes of the jungle according to Peter. My bowl of soup had a chicken wing in it. They gave me a plate with a hot sauce made from charapita peppers, and limes to add to the soup.

I am pretty sure that I had never had chicken soup for breakfast before, and I do believe that this was the best chicken soup that I had eaten in my life. The broth, chicken, noodles, and hot sauce were all perfectly balanced. The grill they used to cook the soup was cobbled together from bricks, and rebar that looked like it had been salvaged from a collapsed building. The pots used to cook the soup were dented and charcoal black, like they had been used for a hundred years. You can't buy that kind of seasoning. I'd go back to Jenaro Herrera in a heartbeat just for that chicken soup.

After breakfast I walked around town, and shot some video. This place was a lot smaller than Iquitos, and like Iquitos there were stray dogs, and cats everywhere you looked. All the people in Jenaro Herrera were welcoming and friendly. This place had an authentic atmosphere that felt like a deeper immersion into the heart of Northwest Amazonia. It was a town free from heavy western influences. I wanted to spend more time exploring this remote jungle town.

A few hours after breakfast, Peter led the group back to the port on the Rio Ucayali, and we loaded into a couple of peque peques (canoes) to head up the river on a two hour ride to Juan's camp on the Aucayacu river. It started raining as we left Herrera. January is the rainy season in Amazonia, and the shortcut through Lake Supey was open, which made the trip much shorter. As we headed upriver against the current, it started to rain harder. The waves were getting larger and larger. This was a dangerous place to fall out of the peque peque. Peter had told the group stories about people who fell into the river, and almost died. A lot of times when Peruvians had accidents on the river, they ended up losing their soul. Peter explained that losing their soul meant that people would go into a deep depression, and become very afraid of everything, even leaving their homes and walking outside. It is hard for them to perform everyday tasks. Most Peruvians will seek the help of a curandero when losing their soul. Peter spoke of it, as if it was a common occurrence in this part of the world.

As we floated up the Rio Ucayali the view was breathtaking. We passed a herd of water buffalo, and I'm wondered if these were the fields where Peter got his magic mushrooms. Peter told a story as we entered the shortcut to the Aucayacu, but the motor was too loud for me to hear what he was saying. The shortcut is a small stream that is dry land most of the year. It's only about ten feet wide, and the peque peque got stuck in a couple of spots. Juan had to get out of the peque peque to help push us. Juan was seventy, but he moved around like a twenty year-old. We were surrounded by a sea of green grass, birds, plants, vines, and one-hundred foot tall trees. I had finally arrived at the rainforest of my childhood dreams.

Peter sat at the front of the peque peque and was chain-smoking cigarettes, and signaling with his arms to the driver at the back. The signals were to let the drive know which way to steer to avoid hitting trees. We passed lots of camu camu trees growing along the Aucayacu. The Aucayacu River is considered the camu camu capital of the world. There seemed to be a good crop of camu camu available from what I had seen at the markets in Iquitos and Herrera. There were a few local families along the river collecting camu camu berries from small boats. I reached out, and snagged a berry as we drifted close to the camu camu trees. I took a bite, and discovered that the camu camu raw berry was super sour. It didn't taste like those camu camu drinks I had in Iquitos, but it also didn't contain a pound of sugar. Camu camu is a super fruit that looks similar to a cherry. It is full of vitamin C, potassium, and antioxidants.

We passed a Matses village, and I waved to a woman and her children sitting in a peque peque as they washed clothes in the river. There were birds everywhere you looked. I saw a couple of caracaras and hawks, a great sign that I was headed in the right direction. The sky was a perfect shade of blue with a few clouds mixed in. I could feel the magic of the jungle.

Lady and Juan's camp appeared as if it was straight out of a dream. Giant acai palm trees lined the river banks, and several thatched roof houses were spread out across the camp. I had arrived at Julio's land, the land that I had read about in *Ayahuasca in My Blood: 25 Years of Medicine Dreaming*. This arrival brought on a great sense of accomplishment. The energy was strong here, and everything felt alive all around you. I wandered around the camp, filming everything I saw. There was an ayahuasca vine growing outside the front of my cabin. I was on cloud nine. I could see why Peter had been visiting here for the last thirty years.

Peter aimed to give his guests the same sense of wonder and awe that he experienced when he first arrived in Amazonia in the middle eighties. He didn't allow the camp to use any electricity or generators during his jungle jaunts. George, who lived at the camp year-round, had a generator, solar panels, satellite television, radio and speakers, and a refrigerator full of cold Peruvian beer, but during Peter's trips there were no modern conveniences available. You were totally off-the-grid with no cellphone reception. The lights around the camp were lamp oil torches just like the lamps they used a hundred years ago, and each guest cabin had a lamp. There we no showers available on Gorman's trips, so you had to bath in the river like they had been doing on the Aucayacu for over a hundred years.

There were several thatched roof huts for the guests to stay during the trip. Each hut had two individual rooms with a common porch/living room area. The rooms were nothing fancy, just a foam mattress, and a mosquito net. There was a small maloka located in the center of the camp. This maloka was a multi-purpose unit that hosted everything from ayahuasca ceremonies to live music and dancing, and as a market to sell goods to the westerners. Peter's team slept in hammocks in the maloka during the trip. They would hang several hammocks from the rafters at night.

Overlooking the river there was an outdoor kitchen with a screened-in dining room with several picnic tables and benches. All the food and supplies were kept in the dining room. There were bags of bread, and enough fruits, vegetables, and dry goods to feed a small army. We would eat like kings for the next week.

I asked Peter about the food situation. "I'd rather be prepared with enough stuff to offer a variety to my team, and my guests, than to say oh no I brought cucumbers, everyone should be happy with that," he said. "Knowing that, are you kidding? People are gonna loose ten or twelve pounds in the next five or six days. And if you loose twelve pounds in five or six days you gonna be really sick. Cucumbers will not do the trick. Cucumbers will not do the trick if you are walking in the jungle. Maybe sitting in a lodge they would, but not the way we are doing it. So, they need some real food in them. They need rice, and they need protein. Lots of vegetables. Lots of fruit. They need some chicken. Good fish. We don't sit around and deep fry it. We don't sit around and smother it in onions and cornmeal, but we do serve good food. It doesn't do anything bad with ayahuasca. In my opinion it's a-okay with ayahuasca."

The kitchen also served as Peter's office during the trip, and he made one end of a picnic table his desk. On the picnic table was bottles of cumalunga (a jungle potion used for protection), agua de florida, pack of Hamilton cigarettes, a little black notebook where he logged every penny that he spent on the trips, box of McCollins tea, can of leche (milk), and a jar of Nescafe. Peter slept in the kitchen on the picnic table during his trips. He would usually slept sitting up with arms folded to one side, so he could lean on them. Occasionally he would lie down flat on one of the benches, but he didn't sleep much during his trips. He considered himself content, if he managed to get a couple of hours of sleep each night.

Our first meal in the jungle consisted of Peter's version of jungle guacamole, a cucumber, onion, and tomato salad with lime juice, beans, rice, papa a la huancaina, and grilled jungle chicken. They poured us chicha morada (purple corn drink), and I was debating if this was the best meal of my life. I felt like Anthony Bourdain visiting the best jungle restaurant in Northwest Amazonia. The New York City chef Peter Gorman had succeeded in bringing his cooking style to the jungle.

After dinner, Peter told us that we had two jobs to do. "Your first job is to bring me a majas, a giant jungle rodent that is considered a jungle delicacy," he said, "These days they hunt majas with shotguns. And after that you are going out in peque peques (canoe) to collect a giant monkey tree frog. But even more important than finding a majas or a frog is for you to get the sounds of the jungle inside your head. You will hear birds and monkeys and animals sliding into the water. Now it's important to hear those sounds because tomorrow night during our first ayahuasca ceremony when you're under the influence of ayahuasca these sounds could be terrifying and unusual. It might make you wonder, "Oh God what is that?" After getting a jungle ride under your belt those sounds will be reassuring not terrifying. They will be friendly because you will know those sounds, and you've already made friends with them, and that is the important part of the ride on the river tonight. There will be no talking during this ride, and there's nothing you have to say that can't wait for two hours. Let the night be the teacher."

The group was led down to the edge of the river to load into peque peques waiting to take us out on the river. The rest of the group got into a peque peque, and disappeared into the blackness of the night. I was left alone with George. I had only just met George, who spoke about as much English as I did Spanish. I awkwardly got into a peque peque, and sat at the front not sure why the others left me. We floated down the Aucayacu a little ways before cutting back into the trees. The only thing that I could really see was the headlamp used by George. The headlamp was needed to look up in the trees to see if there were any frogs. Most of the time we floated along in total darkness. George was paddling, while I was sitting in the front starting to get a little freaked out. I started to feel the anxiety build as we floated along in the dark. We were only on the river a couple of minutes when George started making frog calls. "Bak, Bak, Bak, Bak," George called out.

It was so dark I could barely see my hand in front of my face. George paddled the peque peque in and out of trees, trying to avoid the vines hanging from the trees. George pulled the peque peque next to a giant tree, and shined his headlamp high up in the tree. Out of the corner of my eye I saw something, and when I turned my head there was a figure coming up out of the water. Then suddenly a body, or a spirit, or something disappeared back down into the water. I rubbed my eyes, not sure if that was real or not.

My heart was racing, and after some high anxiety moments, I calmed myself down, and then I started to notice all of the sounds. The jungle choir was in full force on this night. It was too dark to record any footage, but I did record some powerful jungle sounds.
We didn't find any frogs, but I felt more at ease after our jungle initiation. Amazonia had made her introduction, and it wasn't as scary as I made it out to be in my head. George paddled us back to the rest of the group, and we made our way back to camp. When I went to bed that night I felt more connected to the jungle. Peter was right about the jungle sounds, and calling frogs at night on the river. This experience brought back memories of being a kid, and going out with my older brothers varmint hunting, and using tape recordings of wounded rabbits to lure in unsuspecting varmints. Only this time we weren't going to kill our target. This frog hunt was a catch and release operation.

January 15, 2016 - Aucayacu River

This was the seventh day of the jungle expedition, and Gorman and Juan played cards as they did every morning. They played for money, but I'm not sure how much. Card games was a way to pass the time in the jungle. I'm not sure what the game was called, but it was definitely not poker or any game that I knew. Peter sipped on a bottle of aguardiente as he played cards. Some days he drank more than others, but I never saw him get too drunk. His team kept a close eye on the amount of liquor they gave him each day. Peter was well aware of this limit, because he was the one who gave the orders to cut him off after a certain amount. I didn't see Peter drink on the day that ayahuasca was served.

I had reached my limit with the expat and the Danish woman. They had made it clear that they did not want to be in my film, and I reassured them that I understood this multiple times. They repeatedly asked me to not film them, but it seemed like every time I wanted to record a moment with Gorman, they found their way into the shot. I tried to respect their privacy as much as I could, but I had a job to do, and they were not going to stop me from making this movie.

The eighty-three-year-old retiree had not taken any jungle medicines, but he seemed rejuvenated, even swimming out to the middle of Supey Lake. One unforgettable story about the eighty-three-year-old retiree was that he had struggled with sleeping issues his entire life, but he had never attempted to sleep in a hammock until he joined Gorman's trip. Once the man tried sleeping in a hammock, he slept like a baby. He went all the way to Amazonia to find out that he should have been sleeping in a hammock his whole life.

My first trip to South America was life changing, and my mind had been blown so many times by this point that I'd lost count. Two days ago I drank ayahuasca for the first time in the jungle. I had experienced ayahuasca several times back in the United States, but this was my first real ceremony. This ceremony was what Peter called Peruvian style. It was the way Julio Jerena ran ceremonies. Julio was a self-taught curandero who according to Peter, taught his understudies to "take the medicine seriously, but not themselves."

This ayahuasca was the most intense psychedelic experience of my life, and one that I will never forget. Ayahuasca taught me a lot during that ceremony. Several lessons where laid before me: the power of plants, the power of the jungle, and the power I had within myself to change my existence. I had never purged so much in my life. I got stung repeatedly by ants because I wasn't sure if they were real. They were real, and if you stand in the wrong spot for too long, they will attack. Luckily there was plenty of Gorman's Jungle Juice, an after-sting spray, to put on the bites. Jungle Juice was a spray mixture that was given to Peter several years ago by a jungle curandero. The jungle juice was made from a secret recipe, and the only ingredients that I know are camphor and alcohol, and according to Peter, all the ingredients could be found around Iquitos. It stopped the itching almost immediately. Peter had the mixture bottled and labeled Gormans Jungle Juice After Sting. Each guest received a bottle, and this juice was a lifesaver in the jungle.

Peter had everyone meet in the kitchen so he could give us a talk about the sapo session with Pepe. "We're going to do some sapo this morning," he said. "Nobody has to do sapo, if they don't want to. And I'll do it first, so that you see what the physical effects are, and you'll see me down on my hands and knees wishing I hadn't done it, wondering again why I had done it for the x number of times. Sapo is one of the medicines that has allowed the Matses to thrive out here. Not just survive, but thrive out here. It makes them invisible to animals. It gives them an adrenal drip that allows them to hike a hundred or two-hundred miles without needing a full nights sleep, or without needing much to eat, which means they don't have to carry much, so they can cover ground twice as quickly, than if they were carrying weight. It is used by women to find out if a woman is pregnant . . . whether or not it's a male or female fetus. If it's a female they might want to abort it, 'cause if there's too many females they become a weight on the tribe. Um . . . whether or not the fetus is healthy or not, and if it's not then definitely as an abortive. So this has got a lot of uses. In terms of invisibility, the animals in the forest are notoriously bad sighted. Most of them live in hollowed logs or holes in the ground for eighteen to twenty hours a day in the pitch black. They come out at night when it is pitch black, and they only come out at night to try to avoid predators. Now the predators have adjusted, so obviously that's when predators wake up, and that's when predator events happen, mostly at night. But the animals can smell very well, and they can hear very, very well. Now the Matses have learned to walk through the jungle silently, absolutely silently. They are almost jogging, without touching a branch on the ground. Most of their weaponry is just a stick they pick up, and hit an animal on the head with it, or it'll be a bow-n-arrow, you know. It is said in the sixteen hundreds the Mayoruna used blow guns, but they wouldn't know how to make one in a million years these days. So the weaponry can also be a shotgun if they have it. These days they do, but they didn't used to when I first meet them. One or two guys did, but they rarely had cartridges. So if you need to collect three or four boars a day, you got to get real close to those boars to knock them on the head with a club, or put a noose around their head, and straggle them. Even if you got a shotgun, you got twelve boars around a tree eating, the shotgun will stampede the rest, and you're liable to get stampeded as they frantically hear the noise. But if you can get a noose around their neck, and strangle them, that one drops, and the others keep eating. They won't even notice. And you can do three or four of them, now you got plenty of food. Drag 'em away, put 'em over your shoulder, and carry 'em out. Invisibility comes from when they use sapo in copious amounts. It's a cleanser, I'll get to why that's important, what it does among other things is that it pushes all the fat residuals from meat eating through the pores of your skin. And you'll notice after you finish that your skin is kinda greasy, what happened? Even if you didn't physically feel the sweat of it. If you shower or quickly wash after that, you don't have a human smell anymore. So you've effectively become invisible or invisible enough to the animals, so they won't smell you, and that allows you two steps. Two steps closer is enough to bomp 'em on the head. There not really invisible, but for them it's effectively invisible to the animals. In terms of the hiking, the long distance hiking, and the suppressed need for food and water, among the chemicals in sapo, there are seven prominent, a couple of them that turn on an adrenal drip in the human body. Normally, when the adrenal is turned on, you go into fight or flight mode, right . . . when your adrenal is on full, it's fight or flight. Adrenal drip just allows you a little extra juice. So you hike, let's say you hike five miles up and down the hills of the jungle, you're like, 'we need to rest now', but with sapo you're like, 'that was a good rest let's go'. Sixty seconds and you're refreshed, but for several days. If you take four or five dots of sapo in the morning, and four or five in the evening for a couple of days in a row, that hike becomes like nothing. You don't need to sleep. So instead of a four day hike, it's now a two day hike, and you don't need to sleep or carry food. In terms of us, and why would we bother to do this. Those chemicals that make up sapo are bioactive. Bioactive indicates that your body thinks it created them. It doesn't fool your body. It fits in your receptor sites, as if your body created them. Perfect key to unlock your receptor site, and it's a perfect key, which means once your body has had enough of it, it shuts down. There are two opioids, dermorphin and deltorphin, seventeen and thirty-three times more than the best we can manufacture in terms of painkilling morphin, but they both fit perfectly into the receptor sites. So as potential medicine, imagine end-stage cancer you could be taking fantastic painkiller that don't put you to sleep, not addictive. So that your mom could instead of being on a morphine drip for a month, my mom could've been walking around talking to us having a great time, knowing that she is still going to be dead in thirteen days, but she probably would have preferred having another glass of wine and cheese, rather than lying in bed waiting to die. This also has things like sauvagine, bombesin. It will affect the smooth muscle in your stomach, so there will be moments when you take this when you will feel the urge to excrete. You will have your legs under you. You will not be hallucinating. You'll be able to walk to the bathroom. Now our guys are going to watch you, and not let you walk alone anyway, because once in a while you might trip over something, and fall against a tree."

Peter lit another cigarette, and continued, "The way we give it to you is they take a piece of tamishi, and they're gonna burn you. They're gonna scrape away the skin, exposing the subcutaneous layer of skin. And then they're going to take material that's dried on a stick, collected from the frog. Spit on it to reactivate it. Than take a glob of that goop, and put it in the burns marks. Within fifteen seconds, you will start to warm up. You start to say, "Oh my goodness. Oh shit I don't know if I shoulda done this." You know. You question it, then you'll be okay for three or four minutes you'll be like, "Ok I handled this." Minutes five through eleven or so, you'll be gently moving over to the grass, somewhere in the shade. And my team will make sure that you're not sitting on stinging ants. And you'll probably drop to hands and knees. Hands and knees is a descent pose for this or you might have your head on the ground begging us to cool you off, 'cause your heart is beating and you can feel your pulse. Your head is liable to get very warm. And then you're going to feel really lousy. And the reason you're going to feel lousy is because some of the chemicals in this are detoxifying. They're running through all your organs. They're finding all the poisons that you've been hiding places, and they will eliminate those. But for that half an hour your body has to take those poisons to place to be eliminated, and it has to go through your blood again. So you are being poisoned by the same things that your body has hidden. The toxins that you body has tucked away here, and there are now going to be fresh and alive running through you. And it's kind of scary, and it is really hot, and it's really bothersome. Like what's going on here? I'm poisoned. What did Peter do to me? And you are poisoned, but you're poisoned by your own toxins. The net result at the end of it is that you've eliminated five, eight, ten percent of the toxins in your blood. Your veins, and arteries have had a good cleaning. A good enough cleaning that you might get five percent more blood through there than you were getting. Net result of that is five percent more oxygen to the brain, to your eyes, to your senses. Your eyesight will be better. You're hearing will be better, just because you're getting more oxygen there. Right now it's been blocked by the junk we accumulate. Even if you eat wonderful, wonderful food, we still live in a world where there are cars, and toxins in the air. We're stuck collecting those whether we like them or not. So this medicine is going to clean you out on a physical level like nobody's business. It's a painful, annoying, agonizing fifteen minutes. When I say agonizing, I don't mean you're gonna wish you were dead, just . . . but you might. Don't be surprised. It will burn. It will sear. Like everything else in the jungle, it's bravo. They wanna know. If you want me, are you going to pay the price to get me? Do you really want to be here? Like ayahuasca, do you really want to do this? Do you want to do this again? Do you know what's coming? Okay this sapo is going to be the same way. The first time around, if I don't tell you anything, and you can see it, you might just do it. The second time around it's like do you really want to do this again? And the answer is yes, because it's worth the pain from what you'll get out of it. But the challenge is your decision to do it. Nunu, the same thing. The first two in your nose will hurt like bloody hell. Like a shotgun got blown into the back of your head. And whole parts of your nasal that has never had anything, even when you've done cocaine to the ninth degree. No one has blown a gram with a foot long stick to get it up in there. And that's painful, and your eyes are liable to water. You can't breathe for a second. We always do those in two. So you take one and one. You can quit if you want, but the second one and one is not nearly as bad, and the third one and one is nothing."

Today I met members of the Matses tribe for the first time. Peter had been friends with this Matses couple for thirty years. The names of the Matses that we would be working with was Pepe, and his wife Ireni. Peter hired Pepe to provide his guests sapo and nunu during his trips in the traditional style that he was taught as a boy. Peter hired Ireni to show his guests other traditional Matses customs. Early that morning Pepe and Ireni, and their small daughter had arrived at Juan's camp in a peque peque. When Pepe showed up that day he was carrying a spear that was about eight feet long. I had a selfie stick that I was using as a steadicam, so I think Pepe thought it was some kind of weapon. Everywhere Pepe went he carried his spear, and he watched every move I made. Pepe had seen tv crews and cameras before, but he was watching me like a hawk. In fact, a few months before my arrival, ABC's *Nightline News* had visited the camp, and filmed the giant monkey tree frog for a story they produced on sapo in the western world.

Pepe and Ireni communicated with Peter in Spanish, but they made deals with Juan in Matses. Juan was the only one on Peter's team who could speak fluent Matses. Juan had learned the Matses language working in the jungles of Peru many years ago. It was a beautiful morning to experience sapo in the jungle for the first time. Pepe was dressed in a blue tank top, and faded bluejeans that were held up by a red belt. He had on a pair of black rubber boots, and a green baseball cap with a logo that I didn't recognize.

Ruber and Jherman assisted Pepe with making the burns on the guests. Pepe gave sapo to Peter first followed by the other guests, until it was my turn. This was the moment that I had been waiting for, sapo with the indigenous. Pepe had been using sapo as a tool for survival his whole life. He had used sapo to hunt in the jungle, to feed his family, and as the primary medicine to fight off the grippe (influenza).

Notes from my first experience receiving sapo from a Matses medicine man:

We received sapo from Pepe in the morning around nine a.m. My session was very uncomfortable. It lasted forty-five minutes, and I spent most of it rolling around on the ground trying to avoid getting stung by ants. It lasted twice as long as the sessions I had experienced back in the states with Peter. It was a lot more intense with the Matses in the jungle. My arm got hot as hell almost instantly after Pepe placed the sapo on my arm. After the sapo session, we received nunu from Pepe, which I handled way better than the first three times I received the snuff. I dry heaved a few times, but I didn't vomit. I had vomited the first three times I received nunu back in Texas. After this experience with the Matses, I feel like I can build a very good relationship with nunu. I now have a better understand of tobacco's place as one of the master teacher plants. When the session was over, I felt energized. I noticed a difference in my eyesight, and my hearing. I felt really grounded, and connected to the jungle.

January 15, 2016 - Aucayacu River

This was the last day of the trip. There was a party planned on the last night to celebrate all the work we had done over the last week. Peter hired a local band from Jenaro Herrera to come play. Everyone danced and celebrated late into the night.

Peter's team had taken us out on several night trips searching for the giant monkey tree frog, but we never caught one. I was disappointed that I didn't get to film the giant monkey tree frog, but I did capture lots of incredible footage, and now I had a reason to come back. I was leaving the jungle a different person.

8
Piranha Haircuts and Pink River Dolphins

You could drink the truth in its purity if you went to the source.
- John Graves

January 21, 2017 - Iquitos, Peru

I arrived in Iquitos six days before the start of the trip. I had some time to kill, so I decided to brew some ayahuasca. My friend Juan, who I met on my last trip, helped me purchase a bag of ayahuasca vine, and a sack of chacruna leaves. These are the two main ingredients used to brew ayahuasca. Juan took me to the home of a ninety year-old shaman in downtown Iquitos, and the shaman agreed to help me brew the ayahuasca. The shaman's name was Francisco, and he looked like he could be ninety, but you had to take everything you heard in Iquitos with a grain of salt. Francisco and his wife welcomed me into their home like I was their long lost American grandson. Their home was a five minute motorcar ride from the Plaza de Armas.

Today all the guests had arrived in Iquitos. It would be a small group this trip, just four of us.

The guests included a chimney salesman from Massachusetts, a Canadian MMA fighter, and a beautiful blonde world traveler from Amsterdam. The Lady from Amsterdam spoke many languages, and her presence had all the guys falling over each other trying to impress her. I had a crush on her the moment I saw her. I fell even harder when I heard her laugh, and my heart raced uncontrollably when she spoke Spanish to Peter's team. All of us in the group were big personalities, and none of us were backing down from any opportunities to experience the jungle medicines of Amazonia.

The Lady from Amsterdam had developed a sickness from food poisoning upon her arrival into Iquitos, so she asked Peter if it was possible to do a session of sapo. She thought that it might help her condition. I was stuffing my face with a delightful Peruvian breakfast of tacacho, fried eggs, plantains, toast and jam, and washing it down with some fresh camu camu juice when Peter told the group that a sapo session was going down in thirty minutes in his room. So much for fasting before a session with the frog medicine.

Peter's room was in a hotel across the street from the police station. Peter believed this to be the safest room in Iquitos with all the police presence. The local legend was that Mick Jagger once performed on the sidewalk outside of Peter's room for a crowd that had gathered to watch him do a scene for *Fitzcarraldo*.

Peter's friend Dag Walker told me this story on his walking tour on the architecture of Iquitos.

Mick Jagger's character, and his scenes had to be cut from *Fitzcarraldo*, because after many months of delays, Jagger had to leave the film to go on tour with The Rolling Stones. Herzog wrote his character out of the script, because there was no way to recast Mick Jagger. In Les Blank's documentary *Burden of Dreams*, about the making of *Fitzcarraldo*, there is footage of Mick Jagger ringing the bell in the tower of the St. John the Baptist Cathedral in downtown Iquitos. There's also scenes of Jagger acting in *Fitzcarraldo* in the Herzog documentary about Klaus Kinski, *My Best Fiend*.

The building had a colonial rubber boom feel to it. It had to be at least one hundred years old. I entered the outer door of the hotel, and walked down the hallway. Peter's room was the first door on the right. The door was wide open, and the room was full of people. I was the last guest to arrive. As I entered the room, I immediately began shooting footage. The ceiling was thirty feet high. The room was full of plastic bins that contained gear for the jungle trip. There was a desk at the front of the room, and on the desk were bottles of water and Inca Cola, several packs of Hamilton cigarettes, and a bottle of Agua de Florida. There was a chakapa laying in the center of the desk. Several white wooden lounge chairs were spaced around the room. In the middle of the room was a table decorated with the skull of a wild boar, and a giant turtle shell.

Peter sat in a chair holding a plastic bag surrounded by members of his team. He handed a plastic bag to a guy named Keith. Keith had just moved to Peru from Arizona, and was in town doing medicine work. Keith had spent the last twenty years working in the tech industry on the west coast before he answered a calling to go to Peru to work with jungle medicines. He had been doing plant medicine work at Alan Shoemaker's Ayahuasca Medicine House for the past month. Peter had been speaking with Keith that morning at La Noche, and asked him if he wanted to join the session at no charge. "Now you are probably going to puke since you just had lunch, so take this bag," Peter told Keith. "Who else needs a bag?"

Peter handed out plastic bags to the rest of the group. Sidaleth helped make sure that everyone's sleeves were rolled up, and their upper arms were clear of clothing so they could receive the burns. Peter said, "Hey guys this is for those who haven't done it before or maybe you've just done kambo. It's a little different when we do sapo. Kambo is liquefied with water, which simply makes it liquid. Sapo is liquified with spit. My spit, and my spit is really freaking magic. The spit has enzymes, and sugars in it that interact with proteins in the sapo. This medicine takes you to the point where two good dots are usually enough for most everybody. Three dots is a big adult serving. Four dots is show me that you've done it five times. The only person that I've known to do ten is Juan. I did nine one time, and I'll never go back there. Never going to happen."

"Is it like a different animal as well?", asked The Lady from Amsterdam.

"Same animal, but you liquefy with water versus spit, and you drink a lot of water with kambo beforehand with the intention of vomiting. Sapo you don't have the intention of vomiting. You can eat a meal, and you might vomit, but it's not the intention. It's when you feel like doing it, that is when you do it. That's when the Matses would do it. In my world watching kambo people drink two liters of water means the medicine is forced to focus on your stomach area. That's okay, but it is different from what I was taught. What I was taught is that it is supposed to clean you top to bottom. So you don't want to focus on one area. You want it to clean the feathers on your heart when you're older. You want it to clean the plague in your arteries. You want it to clean your kidneys. You want it to clean your liver, so your liver can absorb more vitamins. You want it to clean your lungs, so you can breathe better, not just focus on your stomach. It's a little different than kambo, if kambo is what you've done, in that the burn is bigger, the amount is smaller, but a little more intense." Peter spoke a few more minutes, and then motioned for his helpers to get in place.

I had not filmed a sapo session in Iquitos yet. I had filmed one session in Joshua, and one with Pepe in the jungle, but not one in Iquitos. The Lady from Amsterdam had done kambo before, but she had never experienced the sapo method. The MMA Fighter and the Chimney Salesman were doing it for the first time. The MMA Fighter seemed pretty intense about it, and the Chimney Salesman looked a little unsure, but determined to show his manliness. Keith looked thrilled to be a part of this session. I'm sure Keith had heard a lot of stories about Peter from Alan Shoemaker.

Peter had Juan do the burns. Juan gave burns that lasted a little longer than you feel like they should. I think Juan enjoyed burning the gringos a little too much. After the burns, I sat down to get ready to record audio and video. I hit record on my audio recorder, just before I received the medicine. I received two dots of sapo from Peter. I went first, so I could record the others. The pain was pretty intense, and I remember being glad that I didn't have to use the restroom. The restroom was just a five gallon bucket in a shower in the next room. Most of the group got sick, and were throwing up in plastic bags. A couple of them had to be walked to the bucket in the next room. The Lady from Amsterdam passed out at Peter's feet. Sidaleth fanned a newspaper over her to help cool her off. Peter sang an icaro, and shook his chakapa over her head.

A few minutes after the session was over, The Lady from Amsterdam was smiling and laughing. The food poisoning was gone. The Chimney Salesman and the MMA Fighter were smiling and laughing too. Keith seemed relieved that the experience was over. It was a bonding moment for our small group headed to the jungle. It was a foundation for the work that was ahead of us. On my first trip with Peter, I had only experienced sapo once on the whole trip. I had a feeling that this second trip was going to be much different.

January 22, 2017 - Iquitos, Peru

Juan and I arrived at Francisco's home early in the morning to start the cooking process. Francisco and his wife didn't speak any English, so our talks were limited to my sloppy Spanish. We did enjoy some very nice nonverbal communication with smiles and nodding, even though we didn't have a clue what the other one was saying. I had no idea if this guy was really a ninety year-old shaman or not, because Juan would say just about anything, if he thought it would make him a few extra bucks. Juan had twenty something grandchildren, and he was always hustling. It was best to find him early in the morning before he went to the casinos. Juan was right about Francisco, and I had a wonderful experience brewing ayahuasca in Peru for the first time.

What's the biggest difference between Texas and Peru? It's a question I get asked a lot by Texans, and my answer is that the people of Peru believe in magic. I am not talking about pulling a rabbit out of a hat magic, but the magic of the universe. The magic that I am referring to is the belief that we change the universe through manifestation. Manifestation is something that is brought into the physical reality through belief, intention, thought, feelings, and prayers. And a lot of Peruvians believe that this can be achieved with the guidance of a curandera or curandero.

January 27, 2017 - Iquitos, Peru

Every day for six straight days we have done sapo, mostly in Peter's room, but a couple of times Peter served us at La Noche.

Experiencing sapo in public at La Noche was a much different experience, but the owner encouraged it, and one time she even received a dot herself. Every day we dreaded the sessions, but none of us backed done. The Lady from Amsterdam was always the one who requested it. The Chimney Salesman would ask me everyday if I was doing it again. I couldn't pass up the opportunity to show The Lady from Amsterdam how tough I was. I didn't know a thing about this woman, but I was falling for her fearless attitude towards sapo. If it weren't for her asking for sapo every day, there's no way in hell the group would have continued doing sapo for six straight days.

February 1st, 2017 - Aucayacu River

This was the third day in the jungle, and last night we experienced the first ayahuasca ceremony of the trip. It was very intense, and I didn't think I was going to stop purging. I released a lot of energy last night, things that I didn't even know was there. It's amazing what the body can hide. Rain started pouring down right after the ceremony began as I sat down on a bench next to the maloka. My upper body stayed dry, but my legs got soaked from the rain running off the thatched roof. Jairo's icaros were loud, and strong from inside the maloka.

His spirit looked a hundred feet tall. During the ceremony I experienced flashbacks every few seconds like I was going in and out of this dimension. The flashbacks showed me images of alien spacecrafts. It was a pretty intense early on, and the repeated purging left me outside on the muddy ground most of the ceremony. I found it easier to stay on the ground. Besides the outhouse was closer, if you just stayed outside. Peter's crew had to help me several times during the ceremony. I had George blow mapacho smoke on me several times when the visions got too intense. It finally stopped raining about halfway through the ceremony. The stars in the Southern Hemisphere shined bright, and I could feel the presence of a heavenly spirit watching over us. The Chimney Salesman purged almost the entire ceremony. I had heard a lot of people purge at ceremonies before, but I had never heard anything like the sounds that came out of this guy. This was the Chimney Salesman's first time experiencing ayahuasca, and he was letting out some dark stuff on the jungle ground. His purging triggered loose a lot of deep dark stuff inside of me. After the ceremony was over, I was completely exhausted, but I found the strength to stumble to the kitchen to record a post ceremony interview with Peter. This was the second time that I had interviewed Peter after an ayahuasca ceremony, and I'm not sure how I had the energy to do it. Looking back, I think the making of a documentary helped ground me from some very intense moments with ayahuasca. I had a job to do. I was there to document Peter doing his work in the jungle.

After ayahuasca ceremonies, Peter always made himself available in the kitchen if anyone needed a place to ground themselves, or reconnect, and process some of whatever they just went through. Most of the group made their way to the kitchen, a couple of people went back to their huts. Peter pulled out some crackers, and some delicious Peruvian strawberry jam. We drank glasses of chicha morada, and talked about life until four in the morning. After returning to my little hut, I was serenaded to sleep by the magical bird sounds of Amazonia. As always, I slept like a baby in the jungle.

February 3, 2017 - Aucayacu River

I woke up just before sunrise, and went down to take a dip in the freezing cold Aucayacu. After drying off, I said good morning to Marteen, the camp's pet monkey. Sidalith was cutting up some fish that George had just caught, while the other ladies were preparing to cook a big jungle breakfast after the sapo sessions. I poured myself hot water from a thermos, and mixed in some Nescafe with a little milk and sugar. My favorite time of day in the jungle is morning, because the air is still cool, and there are a lot of birds making sounds. I felt a million pounds lighter after the ayahuasca ceremony. Juan passed around his jar of thirty roots medicine, and I took a big swig. It tasted like the earth.

Peter gave the group a talk about the Matses and sapo. "I wrote those stories in the Matses way," he said. "In the magazines I said that the Matses explained that the frog said when caught "Don't eat me. I'll give you something much better than the food I got, if you don't eat me." So the frog gave them the medicine. Even when you are writing that, and you're copying it down. You realize that's the story that has been passed down. The real version might be that whoever grabbed that frog, immediately got sick, and didn't eat it. Later tried it again, and after a few tries, they felt the after effects of being stronger, of hearing better, and seeing better. They discovered this was some good shit."

Peter and Juan were playing cards when Pepe, his wife Ireni, and their small boy arrived in a peque peque. Pepe and Ireni greeted their friends at the camp as they made their way to the kitchen to see Peter. Pepe was wearing a gray ball cap with NY on it. Pepe smiled at me, and nodded his head as he passed.

This time Pepe gave sapo to the group in the doorway of the maloka. Peter's team was cleaning the mud from the doorway when I arrived. Mud was everywhere from the storm last night. Everyone had to wear their rubber boots, because it was so muddy. There are times in Amazonia when it seems like the rain will never stop. This was the rainy season, and it rained almost every day. Peter went first, and took two dots from Pepe. Then the MMA Fighter stepped forward, followed by the Lady from Amsterdam, and the Chimney Salesman. Everyone had a lot of burn marks from all of the sapo sessions that we had done since that first day in Peter's room.

I came back on this trip again determined to document as much of this experience as possible. I believe that all of those sapo sessions really opened me up, and allowed me to experience one of the most impactful spiritual journeys of my life. I was recording beautiful footage on this trip, and the universe had casted the perfect characters. This trip was a much more pleasant movie making environment that allowed for some magical cinematic moments. I was very grateful to be back in Amazonia.

Peter laid down on the grass under a big acai palm tree, after receiving his dots of sapo. The rest of the group followed his lead, and this was one of my favorite moments of the trip.

After the session everyone gathered back up in the kitchen to refresh themselves with chicha mirada. A couple of the guys went swimming in the Aucayacu. I found a hammock, and tried to get some rest. This experience with Pepe was not as intense as my first session with him, but it was still very strong medicine. I had to stop filming about five minutes into my session. I laid down on the ground in pain, wondering why I subjected myself to such misery.

After the sapo session was over, according to Matses custom, we were offered the opportunity to receive nunu from Pepe. Peter went first, and got two blows of nunu up each nostril. It hit Peter hard, and he started coughing, and spitting up black saliva on the ground.

"Shu, shu, shu." Peter said,

The Chimney Salesman stepped up, and the nunu do a number on him. The Lady from Amsterdam went next, and she got dizzy, and had to lay down. The MMA Fighter took the blows like he was being punched in an MMA fight. I was the last one to go. I thought about not doing it, but you don't pass up experiencing nunu with a Matses. You don't get that many chances like this. We were not just getting nunu, we were also receiving a little Matses spirit when Pepe blew that nunu up our nasal passages, and it was intense. The nunu had a strong effect on all of us that day. Following the nunu session, we enjoyed a delicious jungle lunch prepared by Lady and her kitchen crew. This lunch was one that I will always be trying to top. We had beets, carrots, fresh jungle eggs, jungle fried chicken, papa a la huancaina, and a sliced avocado, onion, and tomato salad.

Peter had a nice surprise for us after lunch. He paid Ireni to cut our hair with piranha teeth. This was the traditional way that the Matses would cut their hair, before they started trading with the western world, and metal scissors were introduced to them. When Ireni was a child she would cut the hair of her father Papa Viajo with piranha teeth, and she had not cut hair this way since she was a young child.

I was the first one to have their ears lowered that day. Right before she was going to cut my hair the bottom dropped out of the sky, and the clouds began pouring rain down on the camp. I admit that I was a little nervous on how the haircut was going to turn out. I handed my phone to the MMA Fighter, and asked him to record my piranha haircut.

Peter began to sing, as Ireni began cutting my hair with the piranha teeth. She held the piranha teeth like a maestro conductor. The teeth gently massaged my scalp as she cut my hair. It felt amazing, and there was a definite technique to cutting hair with piranha teeth. It started to rain so hard that Peter stopped singing. I looked out across the jungle thinking about my family, and how far I was from Jack County. This was by far the most interesting haircut that I've ever received. There's not even a close second. They told me that I was the first gringo to get a haircut the traditional way from this tribe of Matses. The rest of the group got hair cuts too, and the rain continued to come down hard. The rain finally let up when Ireni finished cutting everyone's hair. These haircuts felt like a cleansing moment for our group. Peter said that this was only the second time that he had seen the traditional Matses haircut.

February 4th, 2017 - Aucayacu River

This was the last day of the trip. Last night Peter had been bitten on the hand by an anaconda when he was trying to pull it out of a box. It looked like it really hurt. It made for some great footage for the documentary. Someone had brought the snake to the camp, and Peter bought the snake from them, so they wouldn't kill it. It had been a very eventful trip. Jungle medicines had made us feel like jungle warriors, but after spending only a few hours in the real jungle, it was clear that we were not really warrior material. We spent most of our time out in the real jungle drenched in sweat, and running away from giant mosquitos, and swarms of wasps. This gringo felt much more comfortable back at the camp drinking chicha morada, napping in hammocks, and reading a Richard Evans Schultes book.

I was pretty bummed, because I still hadn't seen the frog. We heard several frogs, but still no face-to-face encounters with the giant monkey tree frog. The main reason that I came back on this trip was to film the giant monkey tree frog. I was starting to think this frog didn't exist. I was extremely frustrated that I had come all the way for the second time, and still no frog.

After breakfast Peter had another surprise for us. Peter told me to go look in a green plastic bucket sitting in the corner of the kitchen. There was a t-shirt over the top of it. I pulled back the t-shirt slowly, not sure what to expect to see in the bucket. Praying to God that it was not another anaconda. It was the most beautiful looking creature I had ever seen. It was a giant monkey tree frog. I felt like Indiana Jones finding an ancient treasure. It didn't look real. The frog sat calmly on a branch at the top of the bucket. It was a bright green color, unlike any green that I had seen before. This frog looked like it was from another planet, and could easily pass for an alien species. It all seemed like a fairy tale. Last night after the party was over at around three a.m., there was a frog calling out not far from the camp. Jaime went out in a peki-peki, and retrieved the frog.

Jaime carried the five gallon bucket containing the frog outside. He began the process of extracting the sapo from the frog by taking a machete, and cutting four small sticks about eighteen inches long. After sharpening one end of the sticks, he placed the sticks in the ground in a rectangular pattern. On the top of each stick a piece of tamishi was tied with a loop to place the frog's leg. The Matses rule is that if you find a frog that still has marks on it's legs, then you should not use that frog for medicine, and you must find another frog. The frogs with the marks haven't had time to store back up a strong secretion in their body since the last time they were milked.

Juan reached into the five gallon bucket, and picked up the frog, and placed it on the Lady from Amsterdam's shoulder. We were all mesmerized by the giant monkey tree frog. The frog's bright green skin really bounced off the Lady from Amsterdam's bronzed arms. I took several photos of the frog sitting on her shoulder with two large rows of sapo burns on her upper arm. This princess had found her frog.

Juan put the frog on top of my head. The village kids laughed at me. The frog didn't move, because it wasn't scared of humans. The frog sat on top on my head for several minutes without attempting an escape. Try doing that with a frog in Texas. These frogs know they will not be harmed. They know the process. I held the frog in my hands for several minutes. It was a full circle moment for me. I was full of gratitude for this universe, for this life, and for this experience.

I handed the frog to the Chimney Salesman, and the frog slowly climbed up his arm. Peter kept telling the group that this is not the way you handle the frog before collecting sapo. Peter said that the Matses hardly touch the frog when preparing it for a sapo collection.

Juan held the frog while Jaime gently placed the loops around the frog's legs. A group of village kids formed a semi-circle around the frog. Jaime positioned each stick so the frog is stretched out looking like what Peter Gorman called a "green trampoline".

Jaime took a small sharp stick, and jabbed it up the frog's nose a little ways to make it uncomfortable enough to secrete the sapo. He then massaged the frog's long middle toe on each foot, and spoke to the frog in his native Matses dialect. After the massaging, he again pushed the small sharp stick back up the frog's nostrils. The village kids were mesmerized by this method of collecting frog medicine. Then Jaime massaged the frog's middle toes a little more. Jaime then took a sharp stick, and scraped the white gooey sapo off the back of the lower leg of the frog. He placed the sapo on a flat piece of wood that was about an inch wide, and a foot long. Jaime scraped across the frog's upper and back legs, and continued the process all across the rest of the frog. Jaime continued the process until he was confident that he had collected enough secretion from the frog. The Matses don't take all the secretion from the frog, so it can quickly build back up its defense system.

The sapo was clear, and looked like glue as it dried on the wooden stick. A Matses sapo stick will usually contain the collection of three different frogs. After the collection, the frog was untied from the sticks. Juan carried the frog to a tree at the edge of the camp, and placed the frog on the branch of a small tree. The frog did not look happy after the process, but it sure beats the alternative of being boiled in a pot or put in a blender. Sapo keeps the giant monkey tree frog alive in the jungle, and not eaten like most animals in Amazonia.

My mission was accomplished. I filmed the frog. We now had a film. There was no movie without footage of the giant monkey tree frog. As we left in the peque peques that day I remember looking back at the camp, and the acai palms one last time, when a pink river dolphin jumped up out of the water. And just before I had a chance to press record, another pink river dolphin glided across the water, and disappeared. I was the only one in the group who saw those pink river dolphins. This was the jungle's way of saying goodbye. It was the perfect exit for my trip back to Texas.

Peter wrote on his blog on 5/8/19:

"Tonight was the first real movie house screening of *More Joy, Less Pain*, a movie made by James Michael McCoy about me, the Amazon I introduced him to, and her rivers, people, and medicines. It was screened at a fancy theater called Alamo Draft House in Dallas, and the theater sat seventy. It was sold out, but because of some really heavy storms earlier in the day, about a dozen people didn't show up. Still, about thirty-five people came for a meet-and-greet with Michael and myself for an hour prior to the screening, and the audience was great when Mike asked me to speak for half-an-hour prior to the screening. I love to talk in public. I love telling stories. I loved telling the audience that I thought they all looked weird when I looked at them naked. I think

I gave everyone a lot of attention during the meet-and-greet, and I think I gave a good, succinct talk about jungle medicines and their value in my life, physically, and emotionally. I didn't go into the spiritual part because that would have taken more time than I had. But I hope I gave generously, directly, and honestly.

I know I get nervous before public speaking. I kid about it but it is real. I went over what I wanted to say half-a-dozen times to myself, to my kids, and was still nervous. And I know that my emotions were high. That proved itself when, on the ride from Joshua to Dallas, Texas, Janis Joplin sang 'Me and Bobby McGee' and I burst into tears. Without drinking wine. And then hell, I started to cry telling a medicine story at the theater. Oh well, if people don't like it, there is nothing I can do. I'm a freaking open book for the most part.

For those who came, thank you. I hope you liked the movie."

9
My Mom and the Frog

Mostly, Texas women are tough in some very fundamental ways. Not unfeminine, nor necessarily unladylike, just tough!
- Molly Ivins

November 26, 2017 - Joshua, Texas

I had been filming Peter for over two years, and shot over three hundred hours of footage already. I was well on my way to assembling a rough cut. I had traveled to Amazonia twice on Gorman's trips, and captured some spectacular footage of the frog. It was time to add some voiceover, and who better to tell the giant monkey tree frog story than the first person to report on receiving the secretion. Peter didn't need a script. He had the words in his head. He just had to grab them out of the ether, and add his New York City articulation.

Peter nailed the voiceover in one take:

"In the Amazon jungle years ago I ran into a group of indigenous called the Matses or the Mayoruna. Among the medicines they use was an extraction from a frog called the phyllomedusa bicolor. Here it's known colloquially as the large waxy monkey frog. It's actually a very small frog that will fit in the palm of your hand. When it's frightened it excretes a solution, a very thick solution that can freeze a snake instantly, before the snake has a chance to close its mouth on the animal. The Matses utilize that solution by burning their subcanteous layer of skin with a small stick to help sharpen their hunting skills, to sharpen their sight, to sharpen the steadiness of their hands with bows and arrows, sharpen their hearing. By chance I would be given some, and my heart raced. I thought my head would explode. I thought I could feel my pulse. I wanted to jump out of my body. I was terrified. I wanted to vomit. I wanted to defecate. I brought that back to some people that I was collecting for at the time. Scientists, and they studied it, and discovered that this medicine contains a number of peptides that interact with the human body as if the human body created them. Now people are using that frog secretion sapo, or by the Brazilian name kambo to cleanse the body. We don't need it for hunting in our world, but we can certainly use it to fine tune our body. Within fifteen minutes of taking sapo, your arteries began to get cleaned out. The plaque is eliminated. Your bioducts began to get cleared out in your liver. Your kidneys get cleaned out. Your lungs get cleaned out. Your stomach gets cleaned out. In short you begin to produce three, four, five percent more blood to your body by the elimination of the plaque, which increases the amount of oxygen going to your organs, which increases the sharpness of those organs.

Over longterm use, this sort of cleanse is like a reset for the entire human body. People who have the gout find out that they don't need to have the gout anymore. People who suffer from swollen feet and ankles due to diabetes discover that their mobility increases. People who suffer from pains, aches, and joints discover that those pains and aches often disappear with regular use of this medicine. It's gotten pretty hip to use it. It's gotten a little overplayed in some quarters as a miracle drug. It's not, but it's darn close to a miracle drug in terms of can it reset the body, so the body has a chance to function the way that it's supposed to, without all the impurities that we take in on a daily basis. Even if we are living with great diets, we still live in a world with cars and exhaust fumes, coal fumes, gas fumes. So we need to get that junk cleared out of us. This is the fastest cleansing avenue. And this ends up being just a marvel at detoxifying your body instantly . . . sapo."

July 18, 2018 - Jack County, Texas

I had assembled a rough cut of the film that was two hours and forty minutes long, and screened the film a few times for friends and family. I received lots of positive feedback. It felt good to finally have a film to show people after three years of working on the project.

My Mom had been very sick in the months leading up to the screening. She had developed some sort of gastronomical infection that western doctors could not identify. She got down to below one-hundred pounds. Her normal weight was somewhere around one-hundred fifty. She was experiencing constant purging every time she ate anything. She ended up in the hospital after six straight days of diarrhea and vomiting. After a week in the hospital she was dismissed, and she returned home, I knew that it was time for her to see the film. I bought a projector, and made a homemade screen with the help of a friend. I wanted her to see the film outside. I felt it would have more of an impact. Mom was so weak that she couldn't walk without assistance. I set up the projector in my parents carport, and we carried Mom's recliner outside so she would be comfortable while watching the film. Mom, Dad, and two of my nieces watched the rough cut.

I had shown my parents some of the footage that I had shot in the jungle, but they hadn't seen any of the edited work. I was really excited to show them what I had been doing down in the jungles of Peru for the past three years. Mom saw the collection of the frog secretion, and the application of sapo in the western world, and how it was being used by people of all ages. She got to see women going through Peter Gorman's sapo training course to be practitioners. My family loved the film, and after the film was over, Mom told me that she was ready to try sapo.

Mom's Life:

My Mom has always been my biggest supporter, and my greatest teacher. She believed in me, even when I didn't believe in myself. I thought I knew a lot about my Mom's life, but when I started asking her about it a few years ago, I realized that I didn't know nearly as much as I thought I did. My Mom, Phyllis Marie Parker McCoy, was born to Roy and Pauline Parker in Loving, Texas in 1943 on Halloween. Loving was a small town of three hundred people located in Young County, about twelve miles northeast of Graham. Loving was founded in 1907 by Oliver Loving Jr., the grandson of the famous cattle driver Oliver Loving, who along with Charles Goodnight developed the famous Goodnight-

Loving Trail to move Texas longhorns back in the 1860s.

Mom had five sisters and three brothers, and she was the fifth of the nine children. Betty Jean, Louise, Patsy, Janie, Phyllis, James, Charlie, Linda Ann, and Ricky Dean was the order in which the Parker children were born. Roy and Pauline got married in 1932 when Roy was 22, and Pauline was 15. Mom said it was a different time back then, and that Granny Parker was a mature fifteen, because she had been taking care of babies since she could walk. Before they got married Roy had made a living hunting, fishing, and trapping wild game. He hunted deer, foxes, rabbit, raccoons, squirrels, and fished for bass, catfish, and crappie. Roy always kept his family supplied with wild game meat. Roy also worked odd jobs like clearing fields, and picking cotton. When he got married Roy sold all his guns, and his hunting gear. He used that money to buy a tent, and he built a wood floor inside the tent, so they wouldn't have to live on a dirt floor. Then he bought a wood burning stove, and a bed. The two oldest Parker sisters, Betty Jean and Louise were raised in that tent.

The Parker's tent was located in Northern Young County, between the towns of Loving and Olney. The Parkers didn't have a car or even a horse. They walked and hitchhiked, if they needed to go into town. Their tent was located near a creek, so they had water if they needed it. After they got married Roy got a job at the WPA (Work Projects Administration). The WPA was a program that was established by President Franklin D. Roosevelt as a relief measure during the Great Depression. Almost everyone was poor, and unemployment caused major issues throughout the state of Texas. During its existence the WPA employed over six-hundred thousand people in Texas paying them wages from fifty to seventy-five dollars a month. These wages helped workers provide food and shelter for their families back home. My Grandfather on the McCoy side, Joseph Claude McCoy also worked for a program created by FDR called the CCC (Civilian Conservation Corps). The CCC pay was thirty dollars a month.

By the time my mother was born, the Parkers had moved into a small house in Loving. My mom was born at home just like her sisters before her. Back in those days it was more common to be born at home than it was to be born in a hospital. The Parkers moved to Graham in 1948. Roy went to work for the state, and he worked for the highway department for thirty-one years. Pauline worked as a cook on the evening shift from three to eleven at a local cafe to help bring home extra money to feed the family.

Graham was founded in 1872 by the Graham brothers who planned to set up a saltworks venture, which later failed because the salt was too expensive to ship. Graham in the late 1800s was the most established town west of Fort Worth, and it became the Federal District Court of Texas from 1879-1896. Then in 1917 oil was discovered in Young County, and the money flowed into town. The oil boom transformed Graham, like numerous other North Central Texas towns, into a place sharply divided between the wealthy and the poor.

The Parkers lived on Victory Street in a working class neighborhood on the Northeast side of Graham. They had chickens, cows, dogs, pigs, even a pet raccoon named Coonus. "Coonus was a good pet until Momma found him eating a cake that she had baked. Momma took Coonus to the park and let him go. James was sad but there was nothing he could do about it, because Momma was the boss," Mom said with a grin, "And Momma would say,'Y'all better find something to do, before I find it for ya' and we'd all run, because we knew if we didn't, we'd be out in the garden pulling weeds or cleaning out chicken houses."

Next to the Parker's home was a big deep creek surrounded by open fields, and pastures. Mom loved exploring that creek with her brothers and sisters. She said that they played outside from sunup to sundown. They didn't have a television, so they had to entertain themselves with lots of games. The sisters used to play with their dolls in the chicken houses, while the boys made guns out of wood. Sometimes they made wood stilts to walk on. Some of the games they played were cowboys and Indians, cops and robbers, dodgeball, hide-in-go-seek, hopscotch, jacks, kickball, mother-may-I, redlight greenlight, red rover, tag, and truth or dare.

At night they would lay out in the yard, and play a game of who could see the first star. They would catch lightening bugs almost every night, because back in those days lightening bugs were everywhere. Mom said they played a game to see who could catch the most doodle bugs. And they would sing a song, "doodle bug, doodle bug come out of your hole and I'll give your bread and honey". She said that their favorite game was who could find the most pee frogs. They would find toads, and put them in a wash tub. Mom had been around amphibians her whole life. Her yard was always full of frogs and toads, and there was always frog statues in Mom's flower beds.

Mom's happy childhood ended abruptly at twelve. That's when she started being treated as an adult. Pauline worked late into the night at the cafe, so it became my Mom's responsibility to get up at five every morning to make Roy's lunch. And since Pauline worked at the cafe in the evening, she had to have dinner ready when Roy got home from work. She also became a mom to the baby Ricky Dean, and her youngest sister Linda Ann.

I asked Mom what they cooked, and she said that most of the time they had fried potatoes cooked in hog grease, and red beans. They made homemade biscuits almost every meal. On Sundays, Granny Parker would cook a big Sunday meal for the family. "Momma was an amazing woman! She was a terrific cook, and she could cook anything. Momma would go out in the yard, and grab a chicken, and ring its neck a couple of times, killing it quickly, and cleanly. Then Momma would cut up the chicken, and fry it. Her favorite part of the chicken was the neck. Everybody always looked forward to Sunday dinners at Momma's. She always had a big garden. She grew black-eyed peas, cabbage, carrots, corn, green beans, okra, peppers, potatoes, squash and lots of tomatoes. There wasn't much that she couldn't grow. She even churned her own butter, and made her own soap," Mom said proudly when asked about Granny Parker.

Then Mom mentioned something that really struck a cord with me. She said that Granny Parker made their clothes out of flour sacks. I had no idea what she was talking about, so I had to do some research. The years following the Great Depression times were rough, and people did not waste a thing. Back in those days, flour came in cotton sacks, and the women would save the sacks, and use the cotton material to make clothes for their children. It was what the poor kids had to wear. The women back then were turning flour sacks into clothing, blankets, diapers, towels, you name it, they could make it out of a flour sack. Granny Parker made all of her kids clothing. There was no other option. Eventually the flour manufacturers got wind of what their customers were doing with the flour sacks, and they started printing patterns on the sacks as a marketing ploy. They made happy mamas all over America with flour sack designs.

I asked Mom if she ever got to go to the movies. "Daddy liked to got to Saturday matinees, but he would only pick one of us to go, because he couldn't afford to take all of us kids," Mom said. "I can only remember going to the movies once or twice, and on Saturday nights all us kids would pile into the back of Daddy's old pickup truck, and we'd go to Louise's because she had a television. Daddy loved to watch wrestling on Saturday nights. I used to get so embarrassed of riding around Graham piled into the back of Daddy's pickup like a bunch of hillbillies. I wanted to play volleyball, but I had to be home to cook dinner for Daddy. I never got to go anywhere or do anything. I got to go to one football game in all my years in school, a homecoming game when I was fourteen."

The Parkers weren't a religious family, so they didn't go to church much, but Mom was Baptized when she was fourteen at the Loving Baptist Church. She told me that they did go to some medicine shows in Graham. Traveling salesmen would set up on the Newcastle highway just down the road from the Parker house, and they would try to sell you different medicines to cure this or cure that. It seems Mom has always been drawn to alternative medicines. Texas has a long history of underground healing rituals such as curing rattlesnake bites by killing a chicken, and wrapping the warm body of the dead chicken around the bite to draw the poison out. Another folk remedy is curing asthma by keeping a small dog in the house so the dog catches the asthma. Some Texans call these rituals 'the old ways'.

The Parkers were one of the last ones on their street to get indoor plumbing. They had an outhouse until the mid 50s, and Mom said that she still remembers the neighborhood boys laughing, and making fun of her because they had an outdoor toilet. I never used outhouses much until I traveled to Peru, but after being in Amazonia, and using outhouses throughout the trip, I fell in love with them. The first thing that I did after I got back from my first trip to Peru was build an outhouse.

Like most middle children Mom felt neglected. She didn't feel like her parents cared whether she went to school or not. She went to school until her sophomore year, when she quit after getting kicked out of study hall because of one of her friends kept talking to her. She never went back. She got a job, and went to work full time. She enjoyed working and being free of the responsibilities of taking care of her younger siblings. Her favorite song at the time was the Roy Orbison song "Candy Man", and soon she found her own candy man, and she left home as fast as she could. Mom married Joe Woolery not long after her eighteenth birthday on January 20, 1962 in Graham. They moved to Olney, where Joe worked at Air Tractor flying airplanes. While living in Olney, Mom had her first two children, Joey and Patty. After a brief time living in Albany, Georgia, Mom moved back to Texas with her children, and filed for divorce in 1972.

She was a single mom working at a sewing factory in Graham when she met another Joe, my Dad, Joseph Claude McCoy, Jr. They started dating in 1972 after seeing each other at a beer joint near Possum Kingdom Lake called The Corral. Things heated up fast, and after three months, they got married. Mom and Dad's favorite song while they were dating was Freddie Hart's "My Hang-Up is You". They lived in Graham for a year, and then moved to Jack County about thirty miles east of Graham.

Mom told me that she was a city girl who had to quickly adjust to life in the country. She said that she was not used to having to drive ten miles to go to the store. My Great- Great-Grandfather, James Alexander McCoy had come to Texas from Alabama after the Civil War. James Alexander was born in 1847 in Tennessee, and moved to Navarro County, Texas in 1868 before moving up to Jack County in 1877. He homesteaded some land in the western part of the county, near a place known as Tater Hill. Like the name says, it's a hill that looks a potato sticking out of the ground. The settlers in this part of Jack County became known as the Tater Hill Settlers. James Alexander married Mary Elizabeth Caddell, and had six children, one of them was a boy they named James Henry, the father of my Grandfather, Joseph Claude McCoy. The McCoys, both James Alexander and his son James Henry, made a living selling cattle. They grew their own food, made their own soap, and only went to town once a month for supplies.

My parents settled onto some land that they purchased from my Grandmother Christine, or MaMaw, as most of the family called her. MaMaw received the land in her divorce from my Grandfather Claude, or PaPaw, as most of the family called him. It was a small section of land next to where my Dad had grown up with his eight siblings. My parents began building their first home in 1975, and I was born on the last day of 1976 at 7:20 a.m. at the Graham Hospital. I was two weeks late, and weighed over ten pounds. My Mom always reminded me of the burden of carrying around that much weight. She told me that she would drink castor oil, and her and Dad would drive down the gravel roads hitting every bump trying to get me to come out. I guess I have always been a little hesitant about sticking my neck out in this world. Eventually, I decided to make my appearance, and my parents got to write me off on their taxes that year. Four years later, my sister Misti was born, and my days as an only child was over.

My parents gave me the choice of going to school at Bryson or Jacksboro. I picked Bryson, which made my parents happy, because that is where my Dad, and my older siblings had gone to school. Bryson is a small town with a population just over 500. The town started out as Mount Hecla in 1878 with just a post office, and a general store. In 1884 the town changed its name to Bryson after Henry Bryson, a man who had built the first log cabin there in 1878. Bryson became the petroleum capital of Jack County when the first oil well was drilled in 1925. Bryson's population peeked in the 40s and 50s during an oil and gas boom, but the population hasn't changed much in the last fifty years.

I went to school in Bryson from kindergarten through my senior year. I played baseball, basketball, and football all through junior high and high school. Mom and Dad were at every game. I could not have asked for more supportive parents. Mom wanted me, and my sister to do everything in school that she never got to do. Mom took us to all the practices, and made sure we had all the equipment that we needed. During my senior year of football she stood up in the stands, and recorded every game I played with a handheld VHS camcorder. Mom was a filmmaker before I was.

One story about her that I'll always remember happened after a basketball game my senior year at Midway. We had a pretty heated rivalry with Midway back then, and the game was very close the whole night. The fans were going crazy on both sides, and we ended up losing by a couple of points. One of the fans from Midway had been cussing and yelling at me all night, and Mom was not happy about that. After the game was over she walked across the court to the Midway side, and poked the loudmouth fan in the chest with her finger, and told him that she did not appreciate the way he was talking to her son. The man apologized, and walked away with a shameful look on his face. Turns out that the man was on the Midway school board, and when Midway came to Bryson to play, he apologized to me before the game. Mom was always sticking up for her children, like the time she went to the school during my eight grade year because she saw lots of bruises on my arms where Juniors and Seniors had been hitting me. I probably deserved it, but Mom didn't care. Those bullies were not going to get away with hitting her son, even if he deserved it; that was her job.

She was always showing us the right way, and making sure we didn't do a half-assed job, as she liked to say. I'll never forget how mad she got at me in the fourth grade because I received an 89 in writing because of my attitude, and that kept me from getting straight A's for the school year. Mom taught me about love and forgiveness, and how to take care of your loved ones. Her biggest pet peeve was lying. You would always get in more trouble for lying than you did for anything else. She didn't like liars or thieves or loudmouths. She was the disciplinarian of the family, and she had several paddles, and was not afraid to use a clothes hanger or water hose. I admit that I needed a lot of discipline, because I was a rebel child who was always questioning authority.

Mom took care of the homeplace, while Dad ran a Caterpillar bulldozer. Dad had a bulldozer business for fifty years. He did mostly farm and ranch work like building ponds and clearing brush, and he worked a lot in the oil patch digging pits, and clearing locations for oil rigs. Mom kept Dad's books, and made sure all the bills were paid. She cooked all the meals, and cleaned the house inside and outside. One of Mom's biggest fears was someone seeing her house dirty. She would not leave the house without making the beds or washing a sink full of dirty dishes. Mom did the family's laundry. You never had to worry about laundry piling up, because she was obsessed with doing laundry. Mom's hard work in the garden and yard taught me how to take care of plants.

Our family might best be described as working class country folks. We didn't go to the country club to play golf. We didn't have lake houses, or second homes in New Mexico, but we lived pretty good. We ate damn good, and we were happy to be living in the country. My childhood was a dream. Me and my best friend Dirk Leatherwood walked all over the hills of western Jack County, and our parents didn't care where we went as long as we were home before dark. It was a time when parents let their kids play out in nature. The freedom to roam the countryside helped me build a relationship with nature, and provided me a sense of independence, and a better understanding of the outdoors.

Mom never once made me go to church or read scripture to me, but she was more of a Christian than any of the holy rollers in our county. She didn't preach to me. She led by example. There was two things that Mom would not discuss or argue about, and that was politics and religion. I think my Aunt Janie might have had something to do with that.

Mom never smoked cigarettes or took pills. She only enjoyed a few alcoholic drinks in her whole life, and I never saw her drunk. The only sickness Mom ever had growing up was the time she got hepatitis as a teenager. The only surgeries she had was a hysterectomy at sixty-five, and a skin cancer removed in her early sixties. She never really slowed down until she reached sixty-nine. That's when her stomach problems started. She went to her family doctor because she had been experiencing severe cramping pains in her stomach. She had diarrhea every time she ate anything. She was enduring episodes of nausea and vomiting and shortness of breath almost everyday. Her doctor had a CT scan done on her, and discovered a calcified irregular mass in her intestines. Her family doctor recommended her to a specialist in Fort Worth. She had another CT scan done in Fort Worth with the same results. Because of the location of the mass, and the difficulty involved with removing it, the specialist referred her to the MD Anderson Cancer Center in Houston. My Mom decided against going to Houston, because that was way too far from home.

All the doctors that she had visited were diagnosing her with a carcinoid tumor. Carcinoid tumors are a type of slow growing cancer that usually begin in the digestive tract. They did a couple of biopsies on the tumor that didn't show cancer, but the tumor was growing, and it was impacting her intestines. She was experiencing acid reflux almost every night, and she was not able to sleep much because of it. She choked on the food that she did eat because the acid reflux had caused her esophagus to narrow which made it very difficult to swallow food. She was referred to more doctors in Wichita Falls and Dallas, but because of the location of the tumor they all told her that surgery and removal was not an option. Basically the doctors told Mom that there was nothing they could do for her condition.

I was shooting footage at the Belen Market in Iquitos in 2016 when I heard Peter mention cat's claw and sacha jergon. I had heard about cat's claw before, but I didn't know anything about it. I had never heard of sacha jergon. Gorman told the group that a tea made from una de gato and sacha jergon was one of the best tumor reduces in the world. At that moment it clicked, and I knew that this was the medicine Mom needed.

Una de Gato or cat's claw is a vine that grows in the Amazon that has hooked thorns that resemble the claws of a cat. It's indigenous to South America and has been used for centuries as a traditional healing medicine to treat a wide range of ailments going back at least two thousand years. The scientific name of cat's claw is uncaria tomentosa. They call it "Life Giving Vine" in South America. The inner bark of the cat's claw vine contains chemicals that boost and stimulate the immune system. The inner bark also contains chemicals that has been used to fight against cancer and viruses. Cat's claw has also been used to help with digestive system disorders, and to improve symptoms of osteoarthritis and rheumatoid arthritis. Some people have reported using cat's claw for treatments on the following health conditions: Alzheimer's disease, cancer, fevers, high blood pressure, anxiety, allergies, viral infections, AIDS/HIV, asthma, bone pains, cleansing the kidneys, cold sores, Chronic Fatigue Syndrome, dysentery, parasites, shingles.

Like sapo, una de gato is not for everyone. There are a few side effects especially when it is first introduced to the body. These side effects can include diarrhea, dizziness, headaches, low blood pressure, nausea, and vomiting. The diarrhea usually goes away with continued use of the cat's claw.

Sacha Jergon is a plant that grows in the Amazon rainforest that closely resembles a snake found in the region where it grows. The name refers to both the plant, and the highly poisonous snake that it looks like. The plant is also used as antidote for the bite of those snakes. Sacha Jergon can help neutralize venom, and toxicity in the body. In addition to being used for snakebites, it has also used for viral infections, and upper respiratory problems. It has been reported in treatments for asthma, chlorosis, menstrual disorders, and whooping couch. The root powder can be applied topically for scabies, and the juice of the plant can be applied externally to treat disorders caused by blowflies. It has been placed in baths to help treat the gout, and applied as a topical wound healer. Sacha jergon has been used to reduce cancerous tumors, heart palpitations, hernias, hand tremors,

HIV/AIDS, and gastrointestinal problems. People in the jungle use it for spider bites, bee and scorpion stings, and other venomous insect bites.

I bought several bundles of cat's claw bark, and a couple bags of sacha jergon root powder to take back to Texas. Peter told us how to make a tea using the cat's claw shredded bark with a tablespoon of sacha jergon the last half hour of a ten hour cook. It costs less than one dollar to make a liter of this tea. It's a really simply method, and if you can make tea, then you can make this medicine.

After I returned home, I made the cat's claw tea with the sacha jergon using Peter's recipe. The cat's claw tea mixed with sacha jergon tasted awful, and I had to convince my Mom that this medicine would help her. I told her that there's an old saying in the jungle that 'the worse it tastes, the better it is for you.' Over the next few months after taking the tea, she started to get better. And after her next CT scan, the tumor was still there, but it was not growing, and it was not impacting her bowels like it was before. The mass in her intestines had stopped growing.

August 22, 2018 - Richardson, Texas

Before Mom watched my documentary, she had already scheduled an appointment with a gastrointestinal specialist in Wichita Falls, so she decided to keep the appointment. And after her meeting with the gastrointestinal specialist, he referred her to a cancer specialist in Richardson. The visit to the cancer specialist in Richardson was one that I will never forget. We waited in a tiny room for what seemed like hours before the doctor came in to visit Mom. The doctor's actions felt mechanical, as if he was going through a routine rather than giving personalized care. He looked at her chart, took her blood pressure, then asked her when she wanted to come in to remove the mass in her intestines. He acted like this was no big deal. It was like he was running a drive-through tumor removal clinic. He wanted to cut her open, and remove a section of her intestines to see if that would help her stomach problems. He didn't know a thing about my Mom other than the few notes he had read on her chart, and he had only asked her a couple of questions before coming up with this diagnosis. I refer to this guy as the joker because he was wearing a purple suit. No way in hell was this man going anywhere near anyone that I loved. As we walked out, the joker told Mom that she was going to waste away if she didn't let him do the operation.

This was the last straw for Mom, and that experience convinced her that western doctors were not going to fix her condition. After we got home, Mom said, "I'm ready to do sapo. What do I have to lose? The doctors won't help me."

She was right. She didn't have any other option. She had done test after test after test, and no western medical doctor could tell her anything. It felt like they were just letting her waste away to skin and bones. She couldn't eat, and her strength was fading. She was getting weaker every day. She needed a miracle, and she needed it fast.

Most practitioners will not serve sapo to anyone over seventy years old. I would not recommend sapo to anyone that was in her condition, but this was my Mom, and I was not ready to give her up yet. Sapo was something that she could receive without leaving her home. I told Mom before we started the treatments that she needed several sessions, and that sapo was not a one time fix-it medicine. We agreed to do it on Sunday mornings.

August 26, 2018 - Jack County, Texas

This was the first day that Mom experienced sapo. We didn't tell the rest of the family about the treatments. And to be perfectly honest I was scared as shit, because I had never witnessed anyone in such a weakened condition receive sapo. And I had never witnessed anyone over seventy receive sapo either. Dad sat in on the session for moral support. Mom was more worried about the burn than anything else. She jumped before I even touched her with the tamishi vine. I only gave her one dot of sapo. You could see an almost immediate reaction in her body. She turned red, and gave me a look of what the hell did you do to me? After fifteen minutes, she was fine. An hour later she was mopping the kitchen floor, and cleaning out her closets. She had not felt this good in many, many years.

October 7, 2018 - Jack County, Texas

Over the last six weeks, she has experienced positive results from her sapo treatments. She had a lot more energy and strength. The diarrhea and the vomiting lessened, and the acid reflux faded. Her balance returned, along with the color in her face. Her attitude was becoming a lot more positive, because she wasn't in so much pain.

A few weeks after her sapo treatments, she returned to the doctor for blood work, and other tests. The results were remarkable. All of her test results came back better than before she had the gastronomical infection. Her appetite was coming back. She began to put weight back on. Her cognitive abilities had improved dramatically, and it was like sapo had set her back twenty years. Mom was back. She was cooking, and cleaning, and going nonstop all day long. Those six Sundays were exhausting, and I was giving all the energy that I had in every session. I am not sure how to explain what happened. It is said that sapo reminds us how strong we are, and it reminded Mom.

There are a lot of people who don't believe it when I tell the story of how sapo saved my Mom's life, but it happened. This is not to say that every person in their seventies should be experiencing sapo, but it worked for my Mom, and it gave her the opportunity to continue living her life.

November 27, 2020 - Jack County, Texas

This was the third Thanksgiving with Mom since she experienced sapo for the first time, and the third Thanksgiving in a row that she cooked, and hosted a meal for thirty-plus people. Mom was in a lot better health since she started working with sapo. She was feeling pretty good at seventy-seven years old. She was still able to do all the things that she did at sixty-seven, just maybe not as fast. She prepared for three days for this Thanksgiving feast. She made eight pies and two cakes. She cooked chicken and dressing, cranberry salad, fried okra, giblet gravy, green beans, sweet potatoes, rolls, and sweet tea. I assisted her, but only following her directions. I would stir this or hand her that, Mom did all the cooking.

April 3, 2021- Jack County, Texas

Mom fried four whole chickens for an Easter lunch of thirty- plus people. She also made four pecan pies, and a banana pudding. She cleaned, dusted, and vacuumed her entire three bedroom house by herself before the Easter gathering. She cooked enough food to feed a small army. She spent three days preparing for this Easter meal. Mom was going strong, and at the top of her game. She was having regular check ups with her western doctors, and the western medication that she has been taking seemed to be working great along with her jungle medication.

September 12, 2021- Jack County, Texas

Mom has been experiencing the same symptoms that she had three years ago. She had been visiting more doctors and cancer specialists. She even had a biopsy done during the second wave of the pandemic. The doctor who performed the biopsy did a terrible job, and she ended up back in the hospital. The biopsy still showed no cancer in the carcinoid tumor in her abdomen. I told her she needed more sapo treatments and a better diet. She had to stop eating fried and spicy food. Mom got down to just above a hundred pounds, before she decided to try six weeks of sapo treatments. It was sapo Sundays again..

May 25, 2022 - Oklahoma

Mom was walking out of a casino in Oklahoma when an automated door hit her, and slammed her to the ground. The impact shattered her right hip bone. Mom was rushed to the hospital, and had emergency surgery to repair her hip with a steel rod. She was back to walking after only a month of rehab. The doctors were amazed at the speed of her recovery.

September 29, 2023 - Jack County, Texas

After her hip surgery Mom was doing pretty well until she injured her finger reaching into her cabinet for some canned foods. The end of her finger started to turn black and blue, and was causing her tremendous pain. We speculated that she might have gout, because she had experienced gout a few years back in her foot. It had been a long hot summer with record temperatures reaching almost one hundred twenty degrees. Sapo had helped her problems, but it didn't make them disappear. Mom decided to try a dot of sapo. After the session Mom felt some relief from the pain in her finger, and she went outside and watered her yard.

November 15, 2023 - Young County, Texas

Mom's finger was not getting better, and the doctors decided to remove the end of her middle finger on her left hand, so the infection would not spread. Mom was in a lot of pain after the surgery to remove the end of her finger. Thanksgiving was only a week away, and she was not going to miss cooking a Thanksgiving meal.

November 20, 2023 - Jack County, Texas

Mom and I did our annual Thanksgiving sapo session to prepare for her four day cooking extravaganza. Not an hour after her sapo session she began cooking her dressing, and all the other Thanksgiving staples that she loved to make like cranberry salad, giblet gravy, and green beans. She also made seven pies (pecan, pumpkin, lemon chess) and three cakes (German chocolate, prune, chocolate sheet).

She ended up hosting over thirty guests for our Thanksgiving meal.

December 20, 2023 - Young County, Texas

After over ten years of visiting doctor after doctor, Mom finally received a diagnosis. She was diagnosed with a condition known as scleroderma, an autoimmune disorder for which there is no known cure. The scleroderma was most likely caused by the mass in her abdomen. The scleroderma caused Raynaud's phenomenon, a disorder that causes damage to blood vessels, and reduces blood flow in the hands, and that is why she had to have the end of her finger removed. She was relieved to finally know what was wrong with her.

November 28, 2024 - Jack County, Texas

Mom and I cooked Thanksgiving dinner for thirty people. We started three days before, and made chicken and dressing, giblet gravy, green beans, cranberry salad, four pecan pies, two pumpkin pies, and a german chocolate cake. One of the best Thanksgiving meals the McCoy's ever had.

January 8, 2025 - Wichita Falls, Texas

Mom left us on a Wednesday at 2:30 P.M. She had developed sepsis from a urinary tract infection, and her health had been declining leading up to her last hospital visit. Twenty-nine years earlier on March 7, 1996 I was living in Wichita Falls, and attending Midwestern State University when Mom called me early in the morning to tell me that Granny Parker had passed away.

Mom had lived a good life, and God was ready to take her home. Her body had overcome a lot in her eighty-one years on this planet. One of Mom's biggest fears was ending up in a nursing home like her father. She always said that she wanted to pass away peacefully in her sleep like her mother. I am grateful to have been there at her bedside to hold her hand as her heart slowly stopped beating.

Jungle medicines extended Mom's life, and gave our family the opportunity to spend several more years with her, allowing us to share many more Thanksgiving, Easter, and Christmas dinners together. We had big parties to celebrate Mom and Dad's 80th birthdays. She watched several more of her grandchildren play sports, and graduate high school. We enjoyed a lot more laughs and smiles with her, and she was able to teach her large family a few more lessons on how to love, and take care of each other. She was the glue that kept our family together. She can never be replaced, and she will be always be remembered for the love she showed us.

I want it to be known that jungle medicines are not the only thing that kept my Mom going the last few years of her life. She also received some excellent care from the North Texas medical community during her several bouts with broken bones, pneumonia, rectal prolapse, RSV, scleroderma, surgeries, and other illnesses. I am grateful for all the nurses, doctors, and healthcare professionals who helped my Mom over the years.

Just like Peter Gorman, her life was made longer with a combination of western medicine and jungle medicine. Both Peter and Mom received all of the recommended vaccinations, and had regular visits with their primary care physicians. I am hopeful that in the future our health care system will evolve into a more open minded community that offers jungle medicines as treatments for certain medical conditions.

This book doesn't lay claim to solid scholarliness, and a lot of the ideas in this book came from the works of others. All of these works played a part in helping me complete this book.

Books:

Peter Gorman, Sapo in My Soul, 2015
Peter Gorman, Ayahuasca in My Blood, 2010
Peter Gorman, Magic Mushrooms in India, 2021
Mark Plotkin, Medicine Quest, 2000
Mark Plotkin, Tales of a Shaman's Apprentice, 1993
Mark Plotkin, The Amazon, 2020
Wade Davis, One River, 1996
Petru Popescu, The Encounter: Amazon Beaming, 1991
Werner Herzog, Conquest of the Useless, 2004
Carlos Castaneda, The Teachings of Don Juan, 1968
Albert Hoffman, LSD: My Problem Child, 1979
Richard Evans Schultes, Plants of the Gods, 1979
Richard Evans Schultes, The Healing Forest, 1990
F. Bruce Lamb, Wizards of the Upper Amazon, 1971
Aldous Huxley, The Doors of Perception, 1954
Terence McKenna, Food of the Gods, 1993
Terence McKenna, The Archaic Revival, 1992
Terence McKenna, The Invisible Landscape, 1994
Terence McKenna, True Hallucinations, 1994
Christopher Ryan, Sex at Dawn, 2011
Giovanni Lattanzi, Kambo Iboga Ayahuasca, 2022
Graham Hancock, Supernatural, 2013
Graham Hancock, Entangled: The Eater of Souls, 2010
Charles Waterton, Wanderings in South America, 1825
Joseph Conrad, Heart of Darkness, 1899
Michael Harner, The Way of the Shaman, 1980
Rian Eisler, The Chalice and the Blade, 1987
Daniel Pinchbeck, Sophia Roklin, When Plants Dream, 2019
Anthony Bourdain, Kitchen Confidential, 2000

John Graves, Goodbye to a River, 1960
Larry McMurtry, In a Narrow Grave: Essays on Texas, 1968
Larry McMurtry, Roads, 2000
Larry McMurtry, Books: A Memoir, 2008
Ida Lasater Huckabay, 94 Years in Jack County, 1949
Thomas F. Horton, History of Jack County, 1933
Candice Millard, The River of Doubt, 2005
Paul Stamets, Psilocybin Mushrooms of the World, 1996
William Leonard Pickard, The Rose of Paracelsus, 2022
Rick Strassman, DMT - The Spirit Molecule, 2000
Robert Greenfield, Timothy Leary: A Biography, 2006
James Redfield, The Celestine Prophecy, 1993
Charles Bukowski, Ham on Rye, 1982
Charles Bukowski, Hollywood, 1989
Charles Bukowski, Post Office, 1971
Charles Bukowski, Women, 1978
Alan Shoemaker, Ayahuasca Medicine, 2014
D.W. Walker, Confessions of an Ayahuasca Skeptic, 2014
John C. Lilly, The Scientist, 1978
William Burroughs/Allen Ginsberg, The Yage Letters, 1963
Ram Dass, Be Here Now, 1971
Ram Dass, Still Here, 2000

Films:
Werner Herzog, Fitzcarraldo, 1982
Werner Herzog, Aguirre, Wrath of God, 1972
Werner Herzog, My Best Fiend, 1999
Werner Herzog, Happy People, 2010
L.M. Kit Carson, The American Dreamer,1971
Lawrence Schiller
L.M. Kit Carson, Africa Diary, 2011
Les Blank, Burden of Dreams, 1982
Dennis Hooper, The Last Movie, 1971
Ciro Guerra, Embrace of the Serpent, 2015
Godfrey Reggio, Koyaanisqatsi, 1982
Charles Burnett, Killer of Sheep, 1976
Francis Ford Coppola, Apocalypse Now, 1979
Eleanor Coppola, Hearts of Darkness, 1991
George Hickenlooper
Fax Bahr
William Friedkin. Sorcerer, 1977
Nicholas J. Polizzi, The Sacred Science, 2011
Raz Degan, The Last Shaman, 2016
Alex Pritz, The Territory, 2022
James Szalapski, Heartworn Highways, 1976
Margaret Brown, Be Here to Love Me, 2004
Tamara Saviano, Without Getting Killed or Caught '16
Errol Morris, Gates of Heaven, 1978
Errol Morris, Vernon, Floriida 1981
George Hickenlooper Picture This, 1991
Rene Pinnell, The King of Texas, 2008.
Claire Hule
Eagle Pennell, The Whole Shootin' Match, 1978
Eagle Pennell, Last Night at the Alamo, 1983
Peter Bogdanovich, The Last Picture Show, 1971
Martin Scorsese, The Last Waltz, 1976
Martin Scorsese, Italianamerican, 1974
Morgan Neville, Won't You Be My Neighbor?, 2018
Dean Augustin, Hey Dillon: Last Great DJ, 2009

Articles:

Herbalgram, Peter Gorman 1951-2022, Connor Yearsley, Number 137, Spring 2023

Erowid, Between the Canopy and the Forest Floor, Peter Gorman, January 1995

Erowid, Omni Magazine, Making Magic, Peter Gorman, July 1993

High Times Magazine, Ayahuasca: Mindbending Drug of the Amazon, Peter Gorman, June 1986

High Times Magazine, Quanah Parker, The Comanche Who Brought Peyote to North America, Peter Gorman, July 1991

High Times Magazine, 50 Years of LSD Interview with Albert Hoffman, Peter Gorman, May 1993

High Times Magazine, Interview with Richard Evans Schultes, Peter Gorman, January 1995

The Guardian, The Ayahuasca King: Man Who Gives Jungle Medicine to Lost Souls, Lance Richardson, March 2017

Texas Observer, The Ayahuasca King's Last Tour, Jeff Prince, June 2022

Podcasts & Radio Shows
Coast to Coast A.M., 1/12/1998, Art Bell
Psychedelic Salon, Lorenzo Haggerty, episodes: 276, 277, 280, 467, 468
Tangentially Speaking, Chris Ryan, episode 321
The Hamilton Morris Podcast, The Origins of Kambo with Peter Gorman, 1/1/2022

Papers:

Toxicon - Volume 31, Issue 9, September 1993, Pages 1099-1111, V. Erspamer, G. Falconieri Erspamer, C. Severini, R.L. Potenza, D. Barra, G. Mignogna, and A. Binnchi

British Journal of Pharmacology, Pharmalogical data on demorphins, a new class of potent opiod peptides from amphibian skin, July 1981 pages 625-631, V. Erspamer, M. Broccardo, G. Falconieri, G. Improta, G. Linari, P. Melchiorri, P. C. Montecucchi

National Academy of Sciences, Deltophines: a family of naturally occurring peptides with high affinity and selectivity for delta opiod binding sites, 1989, pages 5188-5192, V. Erspamer, P Melchiorri, G. Erspamer Falconieri, L. Negri, R. Corsi

International Journal of Developmental Neuroscrience, The Opiod Peptides of the Amphibian Skin, Vittorio Erspamer, Volume 10, Issue 1, pp 3-30, February 1992.

Toxicology Research and Application, Review of the physiological effects of Phyllomedusa bicolor skin secretion peptides on humans receiving kambo, 2022, C. Thompson, M. L. Williams

Lectures:

Terence McKenna, Sacred Plants as Guides: New Dimensions of the Soul, Clairmont College 1991

Peter Gorman's Cat's Claw Recipe

* 3 liters of the best water you can find. Do not use tap water.

* 50 grams of cats claw bark

* Bring water to a roaring boil, then reduce to a low simmer for 10-12 hours. Reduce the water to 1 liter. Let cool, and then strain out the cat's claw bark with a cheesecloth, and funnel into a bottle. Do not refrigerate. Store out of direct sunlight.

* If someone has cancer or tumors or other reasons, add a large tablespoon of sacha jergon powder, and stir in the last half of the cook.

* Drink 1 oz of cat's claw tea every morning.